USE YOUR MENTAL ABILITIES

PART 2

APARNA RAMNATH

INDIA • SINGAPORE • MALAYSIA

ISBN 979-8-89610-281-6

Dedicated to my brother, Late Radesh Manian

CONTENTS

CHAPTERS

SOLUTIONS

CHAPTER 01

LETTER AND WORD ANALOGY

Letter analogy and number analogy are similar. In letter analogy, you will have 3 terms and one blank. The group of letters are said to be 1 term. The blank may be before or after equal to 'sign'. The relationship between first two terms are expected to be the same as between the last two terms. The term in the blank should be selected from the set of 4 options such that the above rule holds good.

The word analogy is also similar. The relation between the 1st & 2nd words will be the same between the 3rd & 4th words, so if the 2nd word is the meaning of the 1st word, the 4th word should be the meaning of the 3rd word. If it is opposite, then this also should be opposite.

In letter analogy, this letter-number relation is used.

A	B	C	D	E	F	G	H	I	J	K	L	M
1	2	3	4	5	6	7	8	9	10	11	12	13
26	25	24	23	22	21	20	19	18	17	16	15	14
Z	Y	X	W	V	U	T	S	R	Q	P	O	N

The arrow denotes forward direction

Corresponding letters:

Letters which have the same positions form corresponding letters: A corresponds to Z, B to Y, C to X, D to W, E to V, F to U, G to T, etc.

Numbering the alphabets: Forward (+), Reverse (-)

Sign	Forward/Reverse	Example
+0	Forward	C D → +0; Q R → +0
-0	Backward	U T → -0; J I → -0
+1	Forward	E G → +1; S U → +1
-1	Backward	P N → -1; D B → -1
+2	Forward	A D → +2; T W → +2

Sign	Forward/Reverse	Example
-2	Backward	V S -2 O L -2

Example: Find the missing term

1. MIFD: XTQO:: ????: JFCA

(a) BXUR (b) OLIG (c) YURP (d) QHSA

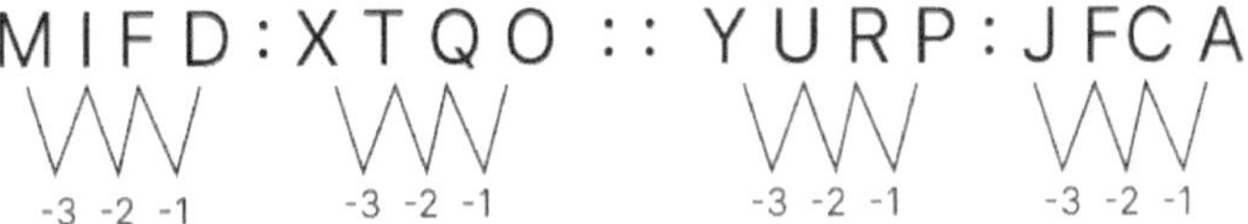

The relation between the 1st set of letters and the 2nd set of letters should be the same as the relation between the 3rd set and the 4th set. So only (c) holds good for rule -3, -2, -1.

Solution: (c) YURP

2. XVTR: ?:: TRPN: GIKM

(a) ZXVR
(b) KMOQ
(c) ABCD
(d) HJLN

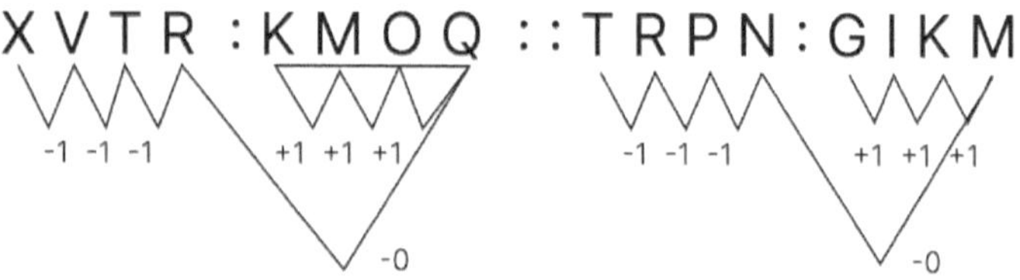

The relationship between N & M from the 3rd set to the 4th set is -0. So the relation between R & Q from the 1st set to the 2nd set is -0. The same rule as between the 3rd & 4th set is between the 1st & 2nd.

Solution: (b) KMOQ

3. ?: AECG:: YCAE: QUSW

(a) IMKO
(b) BFDH
(c) CIEG
(d) WXYZ

The rules followed by AECG, YCAE & QUSW is +1 -1 +1 as shown above. Similarly, IMKO follows the same rule. E&Q between the 3rd & 4th set is +11, and so O&A between the 1st and 2nd has to be +11.

Hence choice (a) IMKO.

4.Protrude: Stick out:: Provender: Fodder

a) Provenance b) Provender c) Provident d) Provincial

Protrude means stick out, provender means fodder.

5. Psychosis: Pertaining to brain:: Pulmonary: Pertaining to lungs

a) Psychosis b) Cardiac c) Diabetes d) Arthritis

Just as psychosis is related to the brain, pulmonary is related to lungs.

Exercise

1. Z A B C: B D F H:: ?: T V X Z

   A) Q R S T B) S T U V C) R S T U D) P Q R S

2. A D G J: ?:: M P S V: O R U X

   A) C F I L B) C Z W T C) Z W T Q D) B Y V S

3. A C E G: Y W U S:: E G I K: ?

   A) U S Q O B) T R P N C) T V X Z D) V X Z B

4. B A C E D: F E G I H:: L K M O N: ?

   A) P O Q S R B) R O S U T C) P I R O T D) Q A R E S

5. M J G D: N Q T W:: ?: P S V Y

   A) B E H K B) O L I F C) Q T W Z D) J G D A

6. B X D V: Y C W E:: F T H R: ?

A) W E U G B) E U G S C) G S I Q D) U G S I

7. A D H N: ?:: C F J P: R U Y E

A) E H L S B) H K O U C) P S W C D) S V Z F

8. Z W T Q: ?:: Y V S P: A D G J

A) B E H K B) A D G J C) Y W U S D) C F I L

9. B Y C X: F U G T:: H S I R: ?

A) V E W D B) F U G T C) H S I R D) L O M N

10. A B C D: X W V U:: ?: V U T S

A) Z Y X W B) Y X W V C) C D E F D) E F G H

11. Y V S P:?:: A X U R: O L I F

A) Q N K I B) M J G D C) O L I G D) N K H E

12. X V T R: Y A C E:: S Q O M:?

A) R T V X B) T V X Z C) R P N L D) P Q R S

13. Impediment: hinderance:: impending: ?

A) Stumbling block B)nearing C) block D) impervious

14. Mortician: undertaker:: Mortify: ?

A) Sullen B) ill humored C) sarcastic D) humiliate

15. Occlude: Shut:: ?: hateful

A) Odious B) odium C) odorous D) ogle

16. ?: woodcutter:: sewing machine: tailor

A) Screwdriver B) Needle C) scissors D) axe

17. Printer: output device:: ?: input device

A) CPU B) ALU C) control unit D) Keyboard

18. Rancor: ?::Recipient: giver

A) Hatred B) bitterness C) love D) Careful

19. Severance: separation:: severity: ?

A) Calmness B) Placidity C) smartness D) Harshness

20. Thrive: flourish:: ?:Strangle

A) Throttle B) Slave C) Torture D) Trouble

21. Wizardry: sorcery:: ?: cunning

A) Wily B) Wince C) Whorl D) Whit

22. ?: Destroy:: Animosity: Active enmity

A) Annihilate B) Annuity C) anneal D) Annals

23. Dilate: Contract:: Dilemma: ?

A) Problem B) Solution C) Expand D) Trouble

24. Table: wood:: ?: Aluminum

A) Sofa set B) T.V C) Aeroplane D) floor

25. Fraught: ?:: Fraudulent: cheating

A) Deceitful B) Filled C) Brawl D) Frantic

CHAPTER 02

LETTER AND WORD ODD MAN

In letter odd man, each set of words will be following a particular rule or pattern. Out of 5 sets of letters, 4 of them will follow the same rule whereas one will not. So that will be the letter oddman.

Even in word odd man, out of 5 choices, 4 of them will be similar in some way or other. One of them will be different. That will be the odd man out.

Worked Examples

(1) A) G J A M P

B) P S I V Y

C) E H E K N

D) D G J M P

E) H K O N Q

Solution (D) DGJMP

All other letter sets have at least one vowel only. (D) has no vowels

(2) A) D L F J H

B) Q Y S W U

C) A I C G E

D) J N K M L

E) O W Q U S

Solution (D) JNKML

In (A),after D alternate letter is F and its alternate is H and its alternate J whose alternate is L

And they come as 1st,3rd,5th,4th and 2nd letters. Similar rule holds good for (B),(c),(E). In (D), J,K,L,M,N

are consecutive letters and are 1st,3rd,5th,4thand 2nd in position. Hence,they do not follow the rule that (A), (B),(C),(E) follow.

(3) 1) MBBS

2) MBA

3) BE

4) ME

5) M.Tech

Solution (3) BE

Only BE is bachelors course, all others are masters courses

(4) 1) R.K.Narayan

2) R.K.Laxman

3) Enid Blyton

4) Sherlock Homes

5) Sudha Murthy

Solution (2) R.K.Laxman

He is the only cartoonist, others are writers

Exercise

(1)	A)	A	B	E	G	I	
	B)	Z	V	R	N	J	
	C)	X	T	P	L	H	
	D)	E	A	W	S	O	
	E)	N	J	F	B	X	
(2)	A)	A	G	L	P	S	U
	B)	U	A	F	J	M	O
	C)	F	I	L	O	R	W
	D)	J	P	U	Y	B	D
	E)	O	U	Z	D	G	I

(3)	A)	B	D	G	K	P
	B)	E	G	I	K	M
	C)	P	R	U	Y	D
	D)	Z	B	E	I	N
	E)	S	U	X	B	G
(4)	A)	D	C	H	F	L
	B)	F	E	J	H	N
	C)	A	F	C	G	E
	D)	J	I	N	L	R
	E)	Q	P	U	S	Y
(5)	A)	E	J	C	G	A
	B)	J	L	H	I	F
	C)	Q	V	O	S	M
	D)	O	T	M	Q	K
	E)	V	Z	T	X	R
(6)	A)	A	J	F	B	E
	B)	I	O	K	J	O
	C)	E	N	J	F	I
	D)	O	X	T	P	U
	E)	U	Z	X	V	O

(7)	A)	C	X	D	W	E	V
	B)	G	S	I	Q	L	O
	C)	H	S	I	R	J	Q
	D)	M	N	N	M	O	L
	E)	U	F	V	E	W	D
(8)	A)	H	E	F	I	D	
	B)	F	C	D	G	B	
	C)	I	J	H	O	G	
	D)	T	Q	R	U	P	
	E)	B	Y	Z	C	X	
(9)	A)	B	F	C	D	N	
	B)	E	F	D	I	O	
	C)	S	D	Z	P	Y	
	D)	Q	M	R	S	V	
	E)	X	G	H	J	L	
(10)	A)	A	A	E	K	R	L
	B)	N I	N	C	H	A	E
	C)	B	B	A	Y	O	M
	D)	E	O	S	M	R	Y
	E)	O W	C N	K	L	U	

(11)	A)	C	O	V	I	D	
	B)	H	E	A	L	T	H
	C)	S	U	M	M	E	R
	D)	F	E	V	E	R	
	E)	N	O	R	T	H	
(12)	A)	D	G	J	N	T	
	B)	P	S	W	C	K	
	C)	K	N	R	X	F	
	D)	B	E	I	O	W	
	E)	E	H	L	R	Z	
(13)	A)	B	E	H	Y	V	S
	B)	D	G	J	W	T	Q
	C)	I	K	M	P	R	N
	D)	T	W	Z	G	D	A
	E)	N	Q	T	M	J	G

(14)

1) G.B.Shah
2) Albert Einstein
3) Isacc Newton
4) Thomas Alva Edison
5) Alfred Nobel

(15) 1) Mobile

2) T.V

3) Telephone

4) Gas Stove

5) Radio

(16) 1) Guitar

2) PlayStation

3) Key board

4) Drums

5) Flute

(17) 1) Chota Bheem

2) Cinderella

3) Snow White

4) Barbie

5) Dora

(18) 1) Ophthalmologist

2) Cardiologist

3) Dentist

4) Teacher

5) Pediatrician

(19) 1) Throwball

2) Ball badminton

3) High jump

4) Basketball

5) Volleyball

(20) 1) square

2) kite

3) Rhombus

4) Pentagon

5) parallelogram

(21) 1) Stockholm

2) Helsinki

3) Brisbane

4) Columbo

5) Tokyo

(22) 1) Wings on fire

2) Swamy and his friends

3) My experiments with truth

4) Letters from father to daughter

5) Paradise lost

(23) 1) Acute angled triangle

2) Rectangle

3) Right angled triangle

4) Isosceles triangle

5) scalene triangle

(24) 1) Mandala

2) Tanjore painting

3) coffee painting

4) calligraphy

5) Kerala mural

(25) 1) Cardiology

2) Mechanical

3) Electronics

4) Telecommunication

5) Data science

(26) 1) Sodium

2) Iron

3) chlorine

4) copper

5) Gold

CHAPTER 03

PYRAMID PUZZLES OR NUMBER TRIANGLES

The problems in pyramid puzzles are following the same rule as number analogy or letter analogy. The shape formed in the pyramid by a set of letters forms one term. The relationship between shapes formed by first 2 terms are same as shapes formed by 3rd & 4th terms. By observing the relation between shapes formed by 2 terms on one side of equal sign the missing term is found out to give similar relation on the other side

Example

d e f g h i j k l m n o p q r s t u v

c b a z y x w v u t s r q p o n m

x y z a b c d e f g h i j k l

w v u t s r q p o n m l k

z a b c d e f g h i j

y x w v u t s r q

j k l m n o p

i h g f e

b c d

a

Choose the correct alternative to fill the blank:

y j i b a: q p e d a:: ?: m l k j q

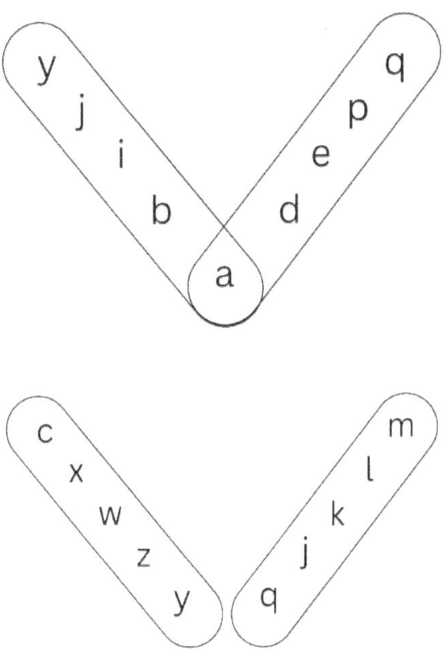

The alphabets on 1st term of LHS are diagonal starting from 'y' ending with 'a' on left-hand side of the letter pattern at bottom. The 2nd term of LHS are diagonal starting from 'q' ending with 'a' on right-hand side of letter pattern at bottom.

The alphabets on 4th term of RHS are diagonal starting from 'm' ending with 'q' on right hand side of letter pattern on top.

So 3rd term on RHS should be diagonal starting from 'c' ending with 'y' on left hand side of letter pattern on top symmetrically opposite to 4th term.

azubw (b) cxwzy (c) nklir (d) mueqe [**Answer-b**]

2) gzaxk: gvatc:: nshqr: ?

lvdrd (b) bxjki (c) fohmj (d) unklm

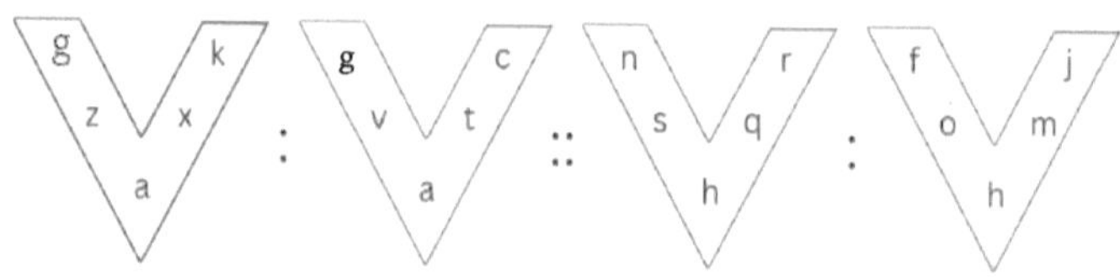

The letters on 1st term of LHS are present in 'v' shape starting from g and ending with k. The 2nd term of LHS are present in 'v' shape below 1st term starting from g and ending with c.

The letters on 3rd term of RHS are present in 'v' shape starting from 'n' & ending with 'r'. So the 4th term of RHS have to be below 3rd term in 'v' shape starting from 'f' & ending with 'j'.

3) xctcx: verev:: tgpgt: ?

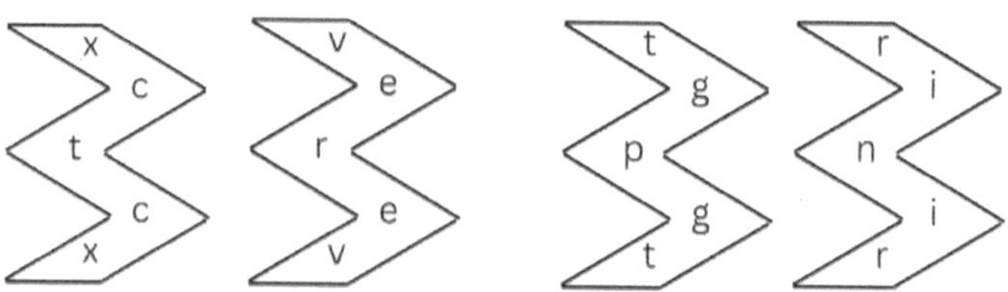

(a) r i n i r (b) k w c s c (c) f q p u n (d) j k l m n

The letters on 1st term on LHS are present in zig-zag pattern as shown above starting from 'x' and ending with 'x'. The letters on 2nd term on LHS are in zig-zag pattern as shown above and to the right of 1st term starting from 'v' and ending with 'v' ie, v e r e v. The letters on 3rd term on RHS are in zig-zag pattern & goes as 'tgpgt'. So 4th term should be to right of 3rd term & will be 'rinir'.

Exercise

I)

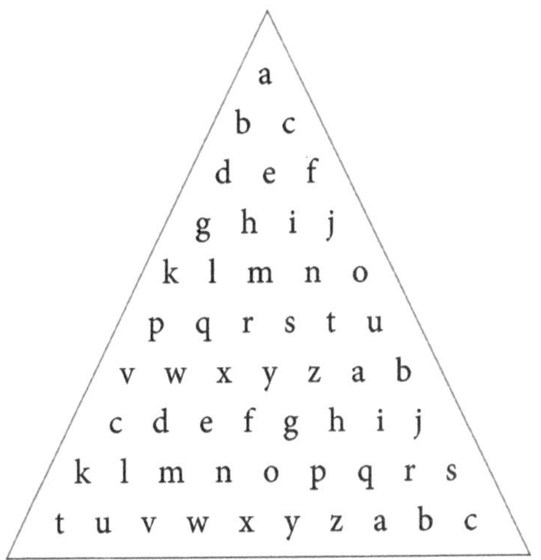

1) p v c k t: u b j s c:: ?: a c f j o

a) d g k p v b) a b d g k c) b d g k p d) c f j o u

2) k p w d m: o t a h q:: l q x e n:?

a) n s z g p b) m s y g o c) n t z h p d) m r y f o

3) ?: c s b r a:: l d m e n: r i q h p

a) u l v m w b) a q z p y c) q h p g o d) t k u l v

4) k c d e f: ?:: t k l m n: c s r q p

a) v p q r s b) j b a z y c) s j i h g d) r I h g f

II)

1

4 3 2

5 6 7 8 9

16 15 14 13 12 11 10

17 18 19 20 21 22 23 24 25

36 35 34 33 32 31 30 29 28 27 26

37 38 39 40 41 42 43 44 45 46 47 48 49

64 63 62 61 60 59 58 57 56 55 54 53 52 51 50

65 66 67 68 69 70 71 72 73 74 75 76 77 78 79 80 81

5) 36,38,62,61,39,35: 26,48,52,53,47,27:: 5,15,19,20,14,6: ?

a) 9,11,23,22,12,8 b) 2, 8, 12, 13,7,3 c) 4,6,14,13,7,3
d) 10,24,28,29,23,11

6) 65,64,63,62,69: ?:: 37,36,35,34,41: 49,26,27,28,45

a) 50,49,48,47,54 b) 81,50,51,52,77 c) 80,51,52,53,76
d) 26,25,24,23,30

7) 17,36,37,63,67: 25,26,49,51,79:: ?: 9,10,25,27,47

a) 1,2,9,11,23 b) 4,5,16,18,34 c) 16,17,36,38,62 d) 5,16,17,35,39

8) 67,62,69,60,71: 79,52,77,54,75:: 62,39,60,41,58: ?

a) 52,47,54,45,56 b) 50,49,52,47,54 c) 51,48,53,46,55 d) 49,26,47,28,45

III)

a b c d e f g h I j k l m n o p q

r s t u v w x y z a b c d e f

g h i j k l m n o p q r s

t u v w x y z a b c d

e f g h i j k l m

n o p q r s t

u v w x y

z a b

c

9) a b r s g: q p f e s::?: d c m l t

a) r s g h t b) g h t u e c) t u e f n d) s r d c m

10) e t i t e: m b q b m:: g v k v g: ?

a) K z o z k b) j y n y j c) h w l w h d) m b q b m

11) t e f g x: ?:: r g h i v: f s r q b

a) d m l k z b) m t s r i c) s d c b o d) e n o p i

12) s g h i u: e s r q c:: ?: c m l k a

a) u e f g o b) h t u v j c) f n o p h d) l t s r j

IV)

100 99 98 97 96 95 94 93 92 91 90 89 88 87 86 85 84 83 82

65 66 67 68 69 70 71 72 73 74 75 76 77 78 79 80 81

64 63 62 61 60 59 58 57 56 55 54 53 52 51 50

37 38 39 40 41 42 43 44 45 46 47 48 49

36 35 34 33 32 31 30 29 28 27 26

17 18 19 20 21 22 23 24 25

16 15 14 13 12 11 10

5 6 7 8 9

4 3 2

1

13) 4,6,14,20,19: ?:: 17,35,39,61,62: 25,27, 47,53,52

a) 1,3,7,13,12 b) 2,8,12,22,23
c) 9, 11,23,29,28 d) 5,15,19,33,34

14) 7,6,5,4,1: 7,8,9,2,1:: 14, 15,16,5,4: ?

a) 13,12,11,8,3 b) 47,48,49,26,25
c) 23,24,25,10,9 d) 12,11,10,9,2

15) ?: 80,83,84,85,86:: 38,63,62,61,60: 48,51,52,53,54

a) 66,99,98,97,96 b) 67,98,97,96,95
c) 17,36,35,34,33 d) 12,11,10,9,2

16) ?: 22,23,11,9,8:: 33,34,18,16,15: 29,28,24,10,11

a) 29,28,24,10,11 b) 20,19,15,5,6
c) 33,34,18,16,15 d) 21,20,14,6,7

17) 96,67,62,37,36: 86, 79,52,49,26:: 94,69,60,39,34: ?

a) 88,77,54,47,28 b) 90,75,56,45,30
c) 91,74,57,44,31 d) 92,71,58,41,32

V)

a

d c b

e f g h i

p o n m l k j

q r s t u v w x y

j i h g f e d c b a z

k l m n o p q r s t u v w

l k j i h g f e d c b a z y x

m n o p q r s t u v w x y z a b c

v u t s r q p o n m l k j i h g f e d

w x y z a b c d e f g h i j k l m n o p q

n m l k j i h g f e d c b a z y x w v u t s r

18) N m w x l k: ?:: w x v u y z: q p d e o n

a) s t p o u v b) m l x y k j c) r s q p t u d) p o e f n m

19) ?: x w z u b:: w v m t a: q d c f m

a) L k j m h b) m l k j m c) v m l o r d) d c x a h

20} e d a b i: o f c h k:: ?: g t m v c

a) e f m h a b) e n u l i c) g p e r c d) s n g l w

21}n m l k j: a b c d e:: ?: n m l k j

a) i h g f e b) r s t u v c) w x y z a d) q p o n m

CHAPTER 04

CHAIN OF LETTERS AND NUMBERS

In this chapter, the numbers or letters are arranged in the form of chain. They need not be arranged in any pattern or using any rule. If alphabets, they ask you to arrange them in a particular manner. After the chain is ready, write your left hand side end of chain as L and write your right hand side end of chain as R and answer the questions accordingly.

Examples

1) Arrange last 13 alphabets in English followed by first 13 alphabets

First arrange the alphabets

L | n o p q r s t u v w x y z a b c d e f g h I j k l m | R

a) Which are the alphabets on either side of 'z'?

1) x,y 2) a,b 3) x,a 4)y,a

Ans: To the right of 'z' is 'a' and to its left is 'y'. so, solution is 4) y,a

b) which is the letter in-between 15th term from right and 18th term from left

1) b 2) a 3) c 4)d

Ans: The 15th term from right is 'y' and 18th term from left is 'e'. The term in-between these two is 'b'. so, solution is (1) b

c) Find the 21st term from right and 4th term to its left. Which is this term?

a) U 2) w 3)x 4)v

Ans: 21st term from right is 's', 4th term to left of 's' is 'w'. so answer is (2) w

d) Which is the letter which is to the left of 10th letter from right

C 2) e 3) b 4) f

Ans: The 10th letter from right is 'd' and the letter to d's left is 'c'. So answer is (1) C

2) Observe this series and answer the questions that follow:

L |5 7 2 8 2 5 5 8 7 2 5 8 8 7 8 2 5 7 8 2 |R

a) How many times does 2 immediately follow 8?

1) 1 2) 2 3) 3 4) 4

Ans: 2 follows 8, three times in the series

b) What is ratio of number of times 5 occurs and number of times 2 occurs

1) 2:1 2) 1:1 3) 5:4 4) 4:5

Ans: 5 occurs 5 times and 2 occurs 5 times.so ratio is 5:5 which is 1:1. So answer is (2)

c) How many 8s occur between 7 and 2

1) 4 2) 3 3) 2 4)1

Ans: 8 occurs between 7 and 2, two times.

d) If 2 consecutive terms are added, how many times is sum 10

1) 4 2) 5 3) 6 4) 3

Ans: The different times when 2 consecutive terms are added to get sum 10 are, 2+8,8+2,5+5,8+2,8+2. So 5 times. Option (2) is correct

Exercise

I) Observe this series and answer the questions that follow

3 3 2 5 1 1 2 7 2 6 8 8 2 9 2 1 2 7 1 3 2 1 2

(1) How many 2s are between 2 odd numbers

a) 3 b) 4 c) 5 d) 2

(2) How many 1s come before 2s

a) 2 b) 3 c) 4 d) 1

(3) What is the ratio of number of times 7 occurs and number of times 2 occurs

a) 1:4 b) 2:7 c) 3:8 d) 4:3

(4) Which 2 of the following occur same number of times

a) 3&2 b) 5&2 c) 7&8 d) 6 & 1

(5) If consecutive numbers are added, how many times will sum be 3

a) 2 b) 3 c) 4 d) 5

II) Arrange first 13 alphabets in English in reverse order followed by next 13 alphabets in normal order

(6) Write the 17th letter from left and 16th letter from right and the letter in-between the above 2 letters

a) a b) o c) n d) b

(7) Count 19 letters from right, to it 4 letters to right. Find the letter.

a) B b) a c) n d) c

(8) How many letters are between 11th alphabet from left and 20th from right

a) 2 b) 4 c) 1 d) 3

(9) Which are the alphabets on either side of 'H'?

a) b&o b) a&o c)o&p d) c&b

(10) Which letter is to right of 13th letter from left

a) n b) a c) o d) p

III) Interchange letters A&B, C&D, E&F and so on till Z

(11) Find the middle term between 15th letter from left and 8th from right

a) O b) Q c) P d) R

(12) Which alphabet is to right of 12th letter from left

a) I b) N c) J d) M

(13) How many alphabets are between 21st letter from left 12th alphabet from right

a) 7 b) 6 c) 5 d) 4

(14) Which alphabet is 4th to right of 12th letter from right

a) S b) T c) Q d) R

(15) Alphabets on either side of L are

a) K&N b) J &I c) J & K d) I &K

IV) observe the following set of numbers and answer the questions that follow

5 2 1 6 3 1 6 2 1 4 3 8 1 2 6 3 7 9 8 1 6 2

(16) How many 1s are followed by 6

a) 1 b) 2 c) 3 d) 4

(17) How many 1s are between 2 even numbers

a) 3 b) 4 c) 2 d) 1

(18) Which 2 numbers occur same number of times

a) 2&6 b) 5&1 c) 1&3 d) 2&1

(19) What is ratio of number of times 8 occurs to number of times 6 occurs

a) 3:4 b)2:3 c) 3:2 d) 1:2

(20) If consecutive numbers are added, how many times will 7 occur

a) 2 b) 3 c) 4 d) 5

V) Write all alphabets of English in reverse order from a to x and write z in starting and y in end

(21) Find the 7th term to the left of 13th term from right

a) T b) s c) q d) e

(22) Find the 11th term from right and 12th term from left and then find the number of letters between them

a) 1 b) 2 c) 3 d) 4

(23) Which is the alphabet on right of 'a'

a) y b) b c) x d) z

CHAPTER 05

NUMBERS IN BRACKETS AND SQUARE CELLS

There are 2 types of problems in this chapter.

Type 1: There will be 3 columns in this type. One column will be in brackets and will be obtained by performing some operations on the other 2 columns. So if column 'a' is bracketed, 'a' will be obtained by some operations performed on 'b' and 'c' (e.g., b + c). So first decode the rule, from the rows already fully filled. Use the rule to fill the blank which is inside brackets.

Type 2: In this type, arrange the numbers in ascending order and see which number series, pattern, or rule holds good. If you find a rule, find the missing number from the rule and fill the blank.

Example 1

a	b	c
8	(2)	4
27	(3)	9
42	(6)	7

Solution: Name 1st, 2nd, and 3rd columns as a, b, and c. It follows rule a/c = b because 8/4 = 2 and 27/9 = 3. So 42/7 = 6.

(a) 5 **(b)** 6 **(c)** 7 **(d)** 8

Option (b) is correct.

Example 2

a	b	c
(7)	81	2
(3)	49	4
(4)	100	6

Solution: Name 1st, 2nd, and 3rd columns as a, b, and c. Rule that holds good is $\sqrt{b} - c = a$. So for the 2nd row, $\sqrt{49} = 7$ and $7 - 4 = 3$.

(a) 1 **(b)** 5 **(c)** 7 **(d)** 3

So option (d) 3 is correct.

Example 3

a	b	c
52	4	12
28	7	19
67	3	39

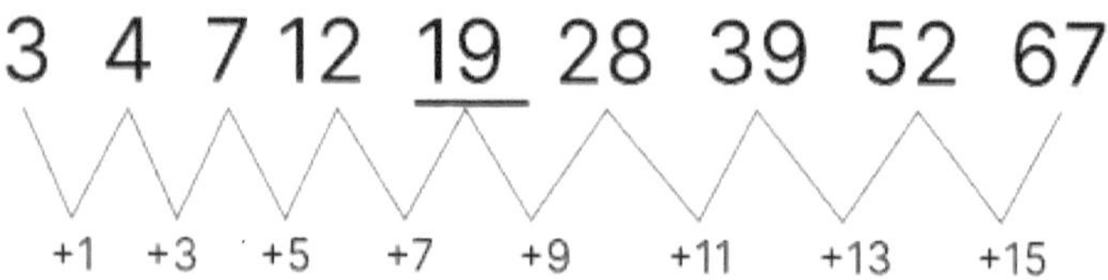

Solution: Write all numbers in increasing order. The difference is in the increasing order of odd numbers. So 12 + 7 = 19, which is the missing term.

(a) 17 **(b)** 15 **(c)** 19 **(d)** 21

So option (c) is correct.

Exercise - Type 1

1.

a	b	c
(__)	72	8
(9)	95	14
(5)	40	15

2.

a	b	c
12	4	(__)
18	3	(12)
21	2	(11)

3.

a	b	c
35	(7)	14
2	(3)	7
55	(_)	9

4.

a	b	c
3	4	(13)
2	5	(11)
6	2	(_)

5.

a	b	c
(7)	8	6
(_)	6	4
(9)	8	10

6.

a	b	c
7	(25)	3
4	(9)	2
3	(_)	5

7.

a	b	c
12	4	(28)
6	5	(31)
15	6	(__)

8.

a	b	c
6	(27)	3
12	(23)	11
10	(__)	8

9.

a	b	c
(40)	7	81
(_)	9	225
(12)	5	169

10.

a	b	c
196	(_)	2
100	(4)	3
81	(1)	4

11.

a	b	c
(_)	3	8
(349)	7	12
(150)	5	50

12.

a	b	c
25	(2)	4
100	(_)	7
400	(6)	3

13.

a	b	c
121	7	(_)
49	5	(6)
9	13	(8)

14.

a	b	c
(_)	121	4
(3)	15	12
(6)	195	21

15.

a	b	c
8	(58)	2
11	(__)	4
5	(7)	6

16.

a	b	c
15	45	74
3	__	9
23	5	33

17.

a	b	c
_	65	5
10	50	17
1	37	82

18.

a	b	c
126	30	2
254	14	_
6	1022	510

19.

a	b	c
59	31	_
41	5	17
2	23	47

20.

a	b	c
998	123	6
25	341	62
_	214	727

21.

a	b	c
1	5040	24
120	6	2
720	_	1

22.

a	b	c
46	80	_
20	34	26
67	22	56

23.

a	b	c
215	612	80
10	927	521
72	_	46

24.

a	b	c
102	_	38
11	74	26
62	12	18

25.

a	b	c
140	91	5
30	0	55
_	204	1

26.

a	b	c
_	259	7
4	19	131
11	35	5

27.

a	b	c
620	800	890
540	750	_
900	690	870

28.

a	b	c
159	11	310
1	41	4
3	_	18

29.

a	b	c
655	592	_
700	637	682
691	616	670

30.

a	b	c
63	15	2
_	82	10
3	50	26

CHAPTER 06

MATCHING SET OF NUMBERS WITH RULES

We have already learnt number series, in which the numbers follow a certain rule or pattern. In this chapter, 5 rules will be given and 5 series of numbers which follow these rules will be given, but not in same order. You should match each series with its rule.

Ex (1)

(A) Add square of no. to double the no.
(B) Multiply the no. by 3 & divide it by 2
(C) From cube of a no. subtract 5
(D) Divide the no. by 2, square the quotient
(E) From double the no. subtract half the no.

(1) 3, 9, 15, 18, 21
$(2 \times 3) \div 2 = 3$
$(6 \times 3) \div 2 = 9$
$(10 \times 3) \div 2 = 15$
$(12 \times 3) \div 2 = 18$
$(14 \times 3) \div 2 = 21$
Ans (1) -> B

(2) 1, 9, 25, 36, 49
$(2 \div 2)^2 = 1$
$(6 \div 2)^2 = 3^2 = 9$

$(10 \div 2)^2 = 5^2 = 25$

$(12 \div 2)^2 = 6^2 = 36$

$(14 \div 2)^2 = 7^2 = 49$

Ans (2) -> D

(3) 3, 9, 15, 18, 21

$(2 \times 2) - (2 \div 2) = 4 - 1 = 3$

$(6 \times 2) - (6 \div 2) = 12 - 3 = 9$

$(10 \times 2) - (10 \div 2) = 20 - 5 = 15$

$(12 \times 2) - (12 \div 2) = 24 - 6 = 18$

$(14 \times 2) - (14 \div 2) = 28 - 7 = 21$

Ans (3) -> E

(4) 8, 48, 120, 168, 224

$2^2 + 2 \times 2 = 4 + 4 = 8$

$6^2 + 6 \times 2 = 36 + 12 = 48$

$10^2 + 10 \times 2 = 100 + 20 = 120$

$12^2 + 12 \times 2 = 144 + 24 = 168$

$14^2 + 14 \times 2 = 196 + 28 = 224$

Ans (4) -> A

(5) 3, 212, 995, 1723, 2739

$2^3 - 5 = 8 - 5 = 3$

$6^3 - 5 = 216 - 5 = 212$

$10^3 - 5 = 1000 - 5 = 995$

$12^3 - 5 = 1728 - 5 = 1723$

$14^3 - 5 = 2744 - 5 = 2739$

Ans (5) -> C

Exercise

I) Match the series with its rules

A. Add half of number with 5
B. Subtract 2 from its square
C. Divide the number by 3 and square it
D. Double the number and minus 4 from it
E. Subtract half the number from square of the number

1. 4	16	36	100	196
2. 33	138	315	885	1743
3. 8	11	14	20	26
4. 32	142	322	898	1762
5. 8	20	32	56	80

II)

A. Divide the number by 2 and add triple the number
B. Add 4 to number and divide by 2
C. Square the number and add half number to it
D. Multiply the number with 3 and subtract product with 5
E. E) Subtract from the number half of the number

1. 7	21	35	49	63
2. 1	13	25	37	49
3. 1	3	5	7	9
4. 5	39	105	203	333
5. 3	5	7	9	11

III)

A. Cube the number and divide it by 2

B. Multiply the number by 5 and divide by 2

C. Subtract the number from its square

D. Add the number with 8 and divide it by 2

E. Square the number and subtract 4 from it

1.	0	12	32	60	96
2.	2	12	30	56	90
3.	5	10	15	20	25
4.	4	32	108	256	500
5.	5	6	7	8	9

IV)

A. Multiply the number with 4 and subtract the product by 5

B. Divide the number with 3 and add 6 to it.

C. Square the number and subtract 1/3rd of the same number

D. Cube the number and subtract 10 from it

E. Add 4 to the number and multiply by2 to product

1.	8	34	78	140	220
2.	17	206	719	1718	3365
3.	7	8	9	10	11
4.	14	20	26	32	38
5.	7	19	31	43	55

V)

A. Divide the number by 2 and square the quotient.

B. Subtract half the number from trice the number

C. Square the number and from it, subtract twice the number

D. Multiply the number by 3 and add 1 to it

E. From cube of the number, subtract 4 times the number

1.	0	8	14	48	80
2.	0	48	192	480	960
3.	5	10	15	20	25
4.	1	4	9	16	25
5.	7	13	19	25	31

VI)

A. Subtract 5 times the number from its cube

B. Add the number divided by 3 to twice the number

C. Multiply the number by 4 and divide it by 3

D. Square the number and divide it by 9

E. Add 1 to the number multiplied by 2

1.	7	13	19	25	31
2.	1	4	9	16	25
3.	4	8	12	16	20
4.	7	14	21	28	35
5.	12	186	684	1668	3300

VII)

A. Add 8 to the number and divide by 2

B. Divide the number by 2 and add quotient to square of number

C. Square the number and divide it by 4

D. Divide by 2 and add 5 to it

E. From cube of the number, subtract 9

1.	0	18	68	150	264
2.	-9	55	503	1719	4087
3.	5	7	9	11	13
4.	4	6	8	10	12
5.	0	4	16	36	64

VIII)

A. Square the number and add same number to it

B. Divide by 2, square the quotient and add 1 to it

C. Divide by 2 and multiply by 7

D. Subtract 2 from number and square the result

E. Cube the number and from it subtract 5 times the number

1.	7	21	35	49	70
2.	0	16	64	144	324
3.	-2	186	950	2674	7900
4.	2	10	26	50	101
5.	6	42	110	210	420

CHAPTER 07

COLORING AND CUTTING OF CUBES

A cube has equal length, breadth & height and is hence a 3 dimensional solid.

Example: Dice, Rubik's cube

Properties of cube:

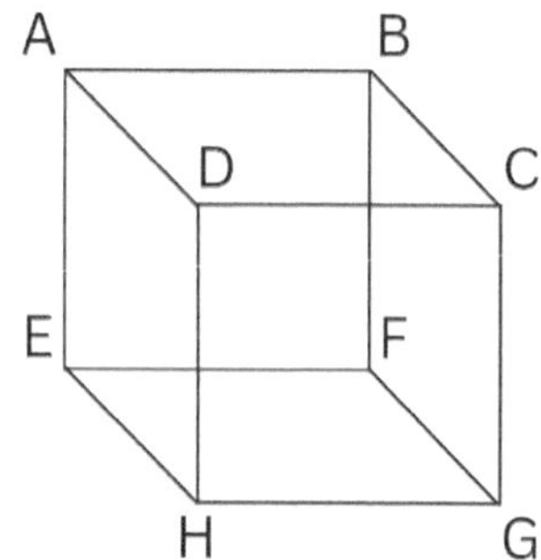

1. Number of vertices - 8 A, B, C, D, E, F, G, H
2. Number of edges - 12 AB, BC, CD, DA, AE, BF, CG, DH, EF, FG, GH, HE
3. Number of faces - 6 ABCD, EFGH, ABFE, BCGF, ADHE, DCGH
4. Number of diagonals - 4 AG, BH, DF, CE

If a cube is painted on all its faces and cut into smaller cubes:

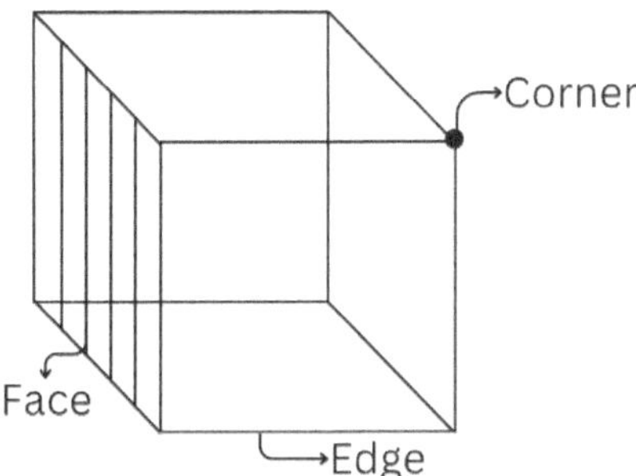

1. The smaller cubes with no face painted are present inside the big cube
2. The smaller cubes with only one face painted are present on the faces of the big cube
3. The smaller cubes with 2 adjacent faces painted are present on the edges of the big cube
4. The smaller cubes with 3 adjacent faces painted are present on the corners of the big cube

Example

1. A cube is painted blue on 4 adjoining faces and yellow at top and bottom. It is cut into 64 smaller identical cubes

a. How many smaller cubes have only one of their faces painted yellow?

(1) 4 (2) 8 (3) 12 (4) 16

b. How many smaller cubes have at least 3 of their faces painted?

(1) 6 (2) 8 (3) 4 (4) 12

c. How many smaller cubes have none of their faces painted?

(1) 12 (2) 16 (3) 4 (4) 8

d. How many smaller cubes have only 2 of their faces painted blue?

(1) 8 (2) 4 (3) 12 (4) 16

e. How many smaller cubes have only one face blue & one face yellow painted?

(1) 16 (2) 8 (3) 4 (4) 2

Solution

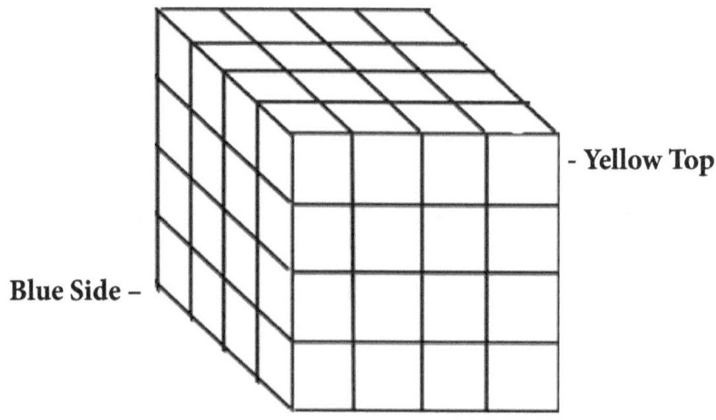

a. At top 4 cubes have 1 face painted yellow & at bottom 4 cubes have 1 face painted yellow. So totally 8 faces.

Ans: (2) 8

b. One cube each at each corner has at least 3 of their faces painted. So there are 8 such corners.

Ans: (2) 8

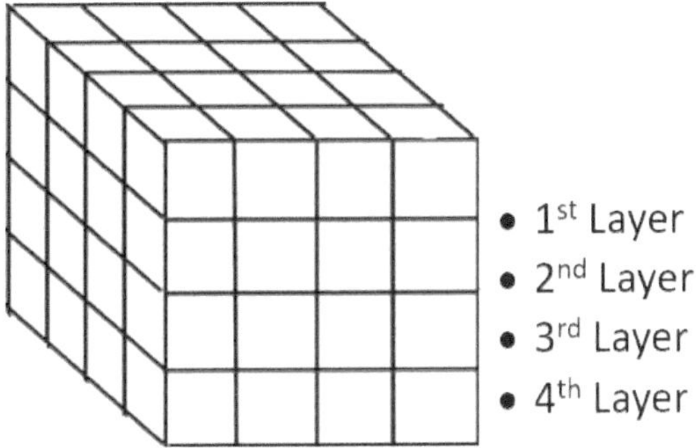

c. In 2nd layer, central 4 cubes will have none of their sides painted. Similarly, in 3rd layer, central 4 cubes will have none of their sides painted. So 8 cubes.

Ans: (4) 8

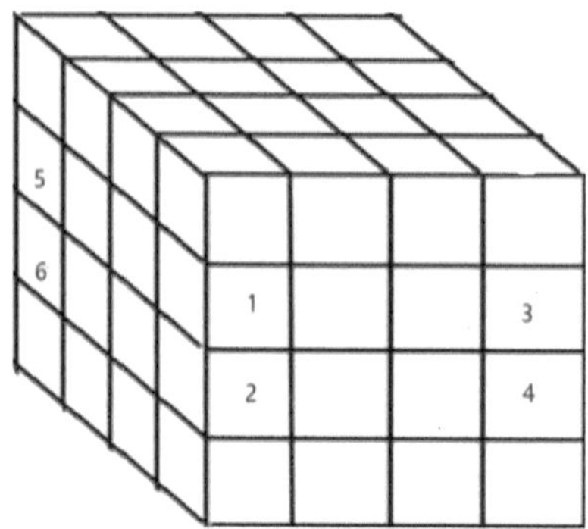

d. Cubes marked 1, 2, 3, 4, 5, 6 have 2 faces painted. Also, 2 cubes diagonally opposite to 1 and 2 faces are painted on 2 faces. So totally 8 faces.

Ans: (1) 8

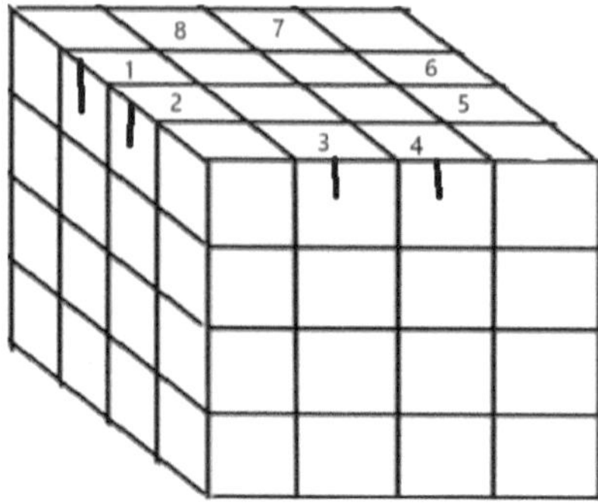

e. On top 8 cubes have one face blue and one face yellow painted. Similarly, at opposite sides at bottom the same 8 cubes have this combination. So totally 16 cubes.

Ans: (1) 16

Exercise

I) A cube is painted pink on 2 adjacent faces and blue on opposite faces. The top and bottom are painted yellow. Cube is cut into 27 smaller cubes of equal size

a. How many smaller cubes have none of their faces as yellow

1) 3 2) 6 3) 9 4) 12

b. How many smaller cubes have at least one of their faces as blue

2) 15 2) 12 3) 9 4) 6

c. How many smaller cubes are painted on only 2 adjacent faces

3) 12 2) 16 3) 24 4) 6

d. How many smaller cubes have one of their face pink and one blue

4) 3 2) 12 3) 16 4) 6

e. How many smaller cubes have at least one of their faces yellow

5) 9 2) 12 3) 15 4) 18

II) A cube is painted with different colors, orange, yellow or brown. No 2 adjacent faces have same color. This cube is cut into 64 smaller cubes of same size.

a. How many smaller cubes have only 3 of their faces colored with different colors

1) 4 2) 8 3) 12 4) 16

b. How many smaller cubes have only 2 of their faces colored with different colors

1) 24 2) 20 3) 16 4) 18

c. How many smaller cubes have only 1 face colored with yellow

1) 0 2) 4 3) 8 4) 12

d. How many smaller cubes have none of their faces colored

1) 6 2) 8 3) 10 4) 12

III) Two equi-dimensional cubes are taken and are joined together. They are painted on all their open faces. One cube is cut into 8 smaller identical cubes and other one is cut into 64 equal smaller cubes.

a. How many smaller cubes have none of their faces colored

1) 8 2) 12 3) 16 4) 20

b. How many smaller cubes have only one of their faces colored

1) 8 2) 12 3) 16 4) 28

c. How many smaller cubes have all 3 faces colored

1) 2 3) 4 3) 6 4)8

IV) In a cube all faces are differently colored. The face painted orange is adjacent to pink face. Blue face faces downwards. The face painted black is between yellow and blue colored faces. The face painted pink is adjacent to the one painted violet. The face painted yellow is opposite to face painted blue.

a. What is the color of face which is opposite to violet face

1) Pink 2) Black 3) yellow 4) orange

b. Which colored face is opposite to one colored black

1) Pink 2) Red 3) White 4) Orange

c. What is color of face at top

1) Orange 2) yellow 3) White 4) Pink

d. Which are the 4 colors on faces adjacent to black colored face

a) Pink, yellow, violet, orange

b) Pink, blue, yellow, orange

c) Violet, orange, yellow, blue

d) Violet, blue, pink, yellow

V) A cuboid of dimensions (5cmX 3cm X1cm) is painted white on 2 of its faces with dimension (3cmX1cm); blue on faces with dimension (5cmX 3 cm) and yellow on faces with dimension (5cm X 1 cm). The cuboid is cut into cubes of dimensions (1cmX1cmX1cm) each

a) How many smaller cubes are formed?

1) 5 2) 10 3) 15 4) 40

b) How many smaller cubes have only 4 faces colored

1) 2 2) 4 3) 6 4) 8

c) How many smaller cubes have 3 of their faces painted with different colors

1) 8 2) 12 3) 16 4) 4

d) How many smaller cubes have only 2 of their faces painted blue

1) 1 2) 2 3) 3 4) 4

VI) A solid cube is painted only on 3 adjacent faces and then cut into 27 smaller cubes of equal size.

a. How many smaller cubes have 3 of their faces colored

1) 1 2) 2 3) 3 4)4

b. How many smaller cubes will have none of the faces colored

1) 2 2) 4 3) 6 4)8

c. How many smaller cubes will have only one face colored

1) 4 2) 8 3) 12 4) 16

d. How many smaller cubes will have only 2 of the faces colored

1) 2 2) 3 3) 5 4) 6

VII) A cube of dimension 3cm is painted orange on one pair of opposite faces, yellow on another pair of opposite faces. The remaining pair of opposite faces is left unpainted. The cube is cut into 27 smaller cubes of dimensions 1cm each

a. How many smaller cubes have no face painted

1) 1 2) 2 3) 3 4) 4

b. How many smaller cubes have 2 faces painted: one orange, one yellow

1) 12 2) 4 3) 6 4) 8

c. How many smaller cubes have one face painted yellow

1) 4 2) 2 3) 6 4) 8

CHAPTER 08

ANALYTICAL REASONING

In this analytical reasoning chapter, the reasoning, analytical and logical skills are tested. The given data is organized in the form of a simple tabular column mostly and inferences drawn from them

Example

Four women, Veena, Jaya, Meena and Tilaka are teacher, engineer, auditor and singer by profession, but not in same order. Each person is with one kid. They go to watch a fashion show.

a. Nitesh, is not singer's son

b. Gayatri is not Jaya's daughter

c. Vijay is not Meena's son

d. Sangeeta's mom is not engineer

e. Tilaka and Jaya were accompanied by their daughters and neither of them is teacher or singer

1. Who is Gayatri's mom and what is her profession?

a) Jaya – auditor b) Tilaka – engineer
c) Veena -singer d) Meena -teacher

2. Who is teacher's kid

a) Vijay b) Gayatri c) Sangeeta d) Nitesh

3. Who is Vijay's mom and what is her profession?

a) Tilaka -teacher b) Veena -singer
c) Meena- engineer d) jaya -auditor

4. Who is Jaya's kid

a) Gayatri b) Sangeeta c) Nitesh d) Vijay

Represent the above information in tabular column as shown below to answer the questions

	PROFESSION				KIDS			
	Teacher	Engg	Auditor	Sing	Gayatri	Sangeetha	Nitesh	Vijay
Veena	x	x	x	✓	x	x	x	✓
Jaya	x	x	✓	x	x	✓	x	x
Meena	✓	x	x	x	x	x	✓	x
Tilaka	x	✓	x	x	✓	x	x	x

1) b 2) d 3)b 4) b

Exercise

I) P,Q,R,S &T are 5 relatives who stay in a joint family. They are architect, contractor, teacher, judge and software engineer but not in same order.

a. R, who does not like football is neither an architect nor a contractor
b. P plays chess but is not a judge
c. Q is an expert football player and not contractor

d. The judge plays good back shots in carom

e. Architect and contractor are not interested in badminton.

f. S does not play carom and is software engineer

g. T swims every Sunday and is a teacher

1. Who is badminton player?

    1) P   b) R   c) S   d) Q

2. What is R's profession

    a) Contractor   b) Teacher
    c) Judge   d) Architect

3. Who is architect

    a) Q   b) T   c) P   d) R

4. Who plays carom

    a) P   b) Q   c) R   d) S

5. What is P's profession

    a) Teacher   b) Contractor
    c) Judge   d) Software engineer

II) Five men Rahul, Kumar, Satish, Anand and Sujay are Lecturer, Auditor, Dentist and 2 others are Engineers. Their wives are Dentist, Teacher, Artist, dancer and singer but not in that order.

a. Dancer is not Rahul's or Satish's wife. Her husband is a lecturer.

b. Sujay is not Dentist

c. One husband and wife have same profession

d. Rahul and Kumar are not engineers and they are not married to either to dentist or artist

e. Satish is not auditor and auditor's wife is teacher

f. Anand and Sujay are neither auditor nor lecturer and their wives are neither singer or teacher

6. Who is in dentists profession with his wife

a) Rahul b) Kumar
c) Satish d) Anand e) Sujay

7. Who is the husband of teacher

a) Rahul b)Satish c) Sujay
d) Kumar e) Anand

8. Who is husband of singer

a) Lecturer b) Dentist c) auditor
d) Engineer e) cannot be determined

9. Who's wife is dancer

a) Rahul b) Anand c) Kumar
d) Sujay e) Satish

10. Which is correct combination of husband-wife?

a) Rahul- dancer b) Satish-singer
c) Anand-artist d) Kumar-teacher e) None

III) For a project,3 R&D engineers, X, Y, Z are selected along with 4 hardware engineers, R,S,T,U. It is necessary that the members must be friendly with each other. The team should have 2 R&D members and 2 hardware engineers

R & S are not friendly

Y & R are not friendly

Z & T are not friendly

11. If Y&Z are selected, the other members of team are

a) Both S&U b) T&U
c) only T d) Both R&S

12. If R is in team, who are the other engineers in team

a) X,Y,T b) X,Z,U c) S,X,Z d) Y,Z,T

13. If S also is not friendly with R & Y, then the other 3 members have to be

a) Z,S,T b) T,S,X c) X,T,U d) X,S,U

IV) There are 5 lecturers A,B,C,D,E and 6 CAS K,L,M,N,O,P and 4 singers 5,6,7,8.

a) Among them, A,B,5,6,M,N,O are females and others are males

b) There will be no female lecturer whenever there is male singer

c) There will be no female CA whenever there is male lecturer

14. If the team consists of 2 lecturers, 2 singers and 2 CAs, all the below teams are possible except

a) A,B,5,6,L,P b) D,E,7,8,M,N
c) C,D,7,8,K,L d) A,B,5,6,N,O

15. If the team consists of 2 lecturers, 1 singer and 3 Cas, all the teams are possible, except

a) D,E,8,K,L,P b) C,D,7,P,L,K
c) D,A,7,M,N,O d) A,B,5,K,O,M

16. If the team consists of 3 lecturers, 1 male singer and 2 CAs, the members of the team can be

a) ABC,7,MO b) BCD,5,LO
c) ADE, 6, MD d) CDE,8,KL

17. If the team consists of 2 lecturers, 1 female CA and 2 singers, the members of team are

a) AB,M,56 b) CD,N,78
c) AC,O,75 d) CE,L,67

18. If the team consists of 2 lecturers, 2 female Cas and 2 singers, all the following teams are possible,except

a) AB,MN,56 b) AB,NO,78
c) BA,OM,65 d) AB,NO,56

V) A jeweller has 5 bangles 1,2,3,4,5 with different weights

1. Bangle 5 is weighing less than 1 but more than bangle 3
2. Bangle 4 is weighing half as much as bangle 5

3. Bangle 3 is weighing half as much as bangle 4
4. Bangle 2 is weighing 4 and ½ times as much as bangle 3
5. Bangle 1 is weighing twice as much as bangle 2

19) Which of the following represents the descending order of weights of bangles

a) 1,2,4,5,3 b) 2,4,5,1,3
c) 5,3,4,1,2 d) 3,1,4,2,5
e) 1,2,5,4,3

20) Bangle 5 is lighter in weight than which of the other 2 bangles

a) 4,3 b) 1,2 c) 1,3 d) 4,2 e) 2,4

21) If these bangles are priced according to weights, which bangle is least priced

a) bangle 1 b) bangle 2 c) bangle 3
d) bangle 4 e) bangle 5

22) which bangle is heaviest?

a) Bangle 1 b) Bangle 2 c) Bangle 3
d) Bangle 4 e) Bangle 5

23) Bangle 5 is heavier than which of the following 2 bangles

a) 4,2 b) 4,3 c) 1,3 d) 1,2 e) 2,4

CHAPTER 09

CUBE FOLDING

Introduction

In this chapter, the nets of cubes are given; if these nets are folded to form cubes, certain faces will be opposite to each other. How to segregate these opposite faces right in the net. Is what you are going to learn, In this are mainly 2 skills:

1. The alternate squares in net are opposite faces.
2. The squares which occur at end of Z i.e at end of Z in many directions i.e, └┐ or ┌┘ or ┐└ etc are opposite faces.

Examples

Identify the pair of opposite faces in Cube if it is:

1.

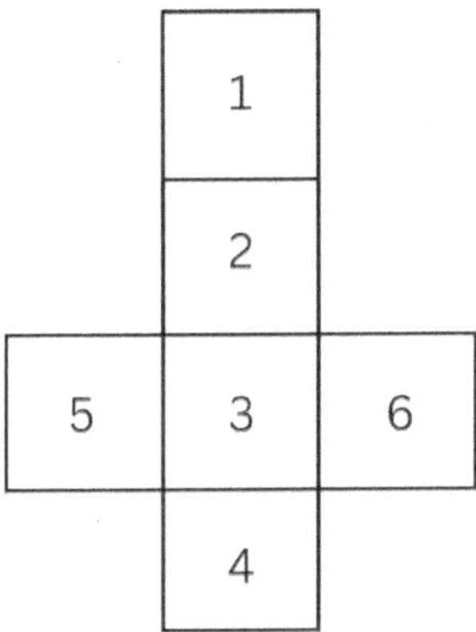

1. 1 and 3 are alternate boxes; 2 and 4 are alternate boxes and 5 & 6 are alternate boxes ⟶ so are opposite faces

a. 1, 4; 5, 2; 3,6

b. 1, 2; 3,5; 6, 4

c. 1, 3; 2,4; 5, 6

d. 4, 5; 3,2; 1, 6

So, the answer is option (c).

2.

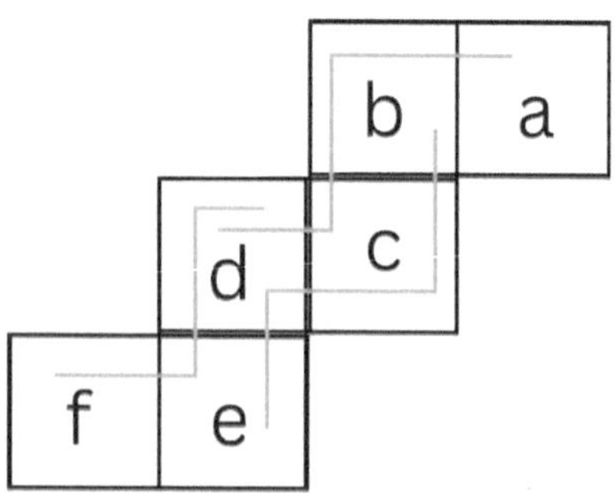

Since at end of ┘┌ a & d occur at end of ┌┘, b & e occur and at end of ┌┘ c & f occur, they form opposite faces

a. a, d; b, e; c, f

b. b, c; d, e; a, f

c. a, c; b, e; d, f

d. d, c; b, a; f, e

So option (a) is correct.

Exercise

In the net of cubes, identify the pair of opposite faces.

1.

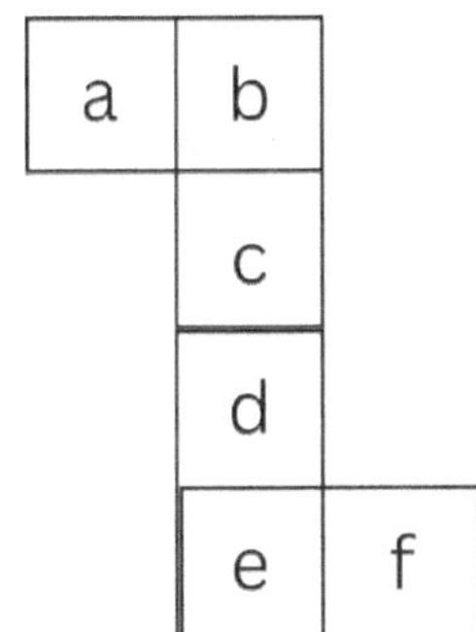

a. b,c; d,e; a,f

b. a, b; c, d; e, f

c. a, f; b, d; c, e

d. a, c; b, d; e, f

2.

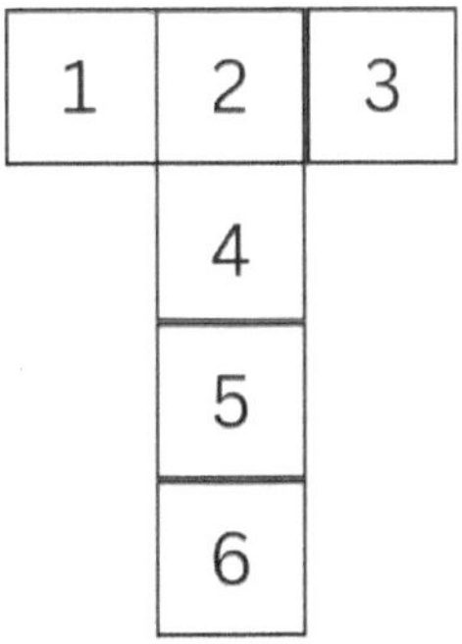

1 2 3
4
5
6

a. 1, 3; 2, 5; 4, 6

b. 1, 2; 3, 4; 5, 6

c. 1, 4; 2, 3; 5, 6

d. 1, 3; 2, 4; 5, 6

3.

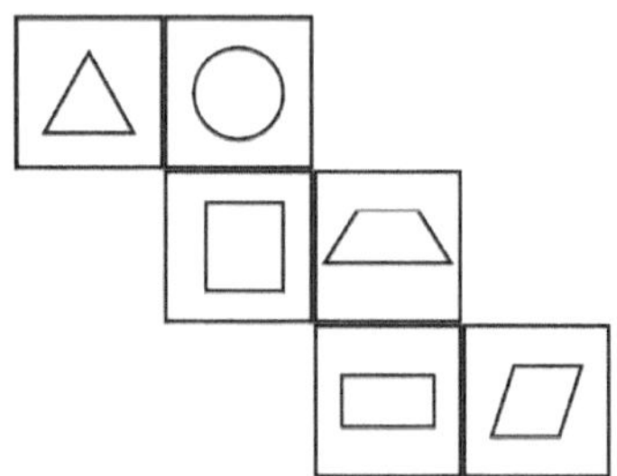

(a) △,○;□,⏢;▭,▱
(b) △,⏢;○,▭;□,▱
(c) △,□;○,⏢;▭,▱
(d) △,▱;○,▭;□,⏢

4.

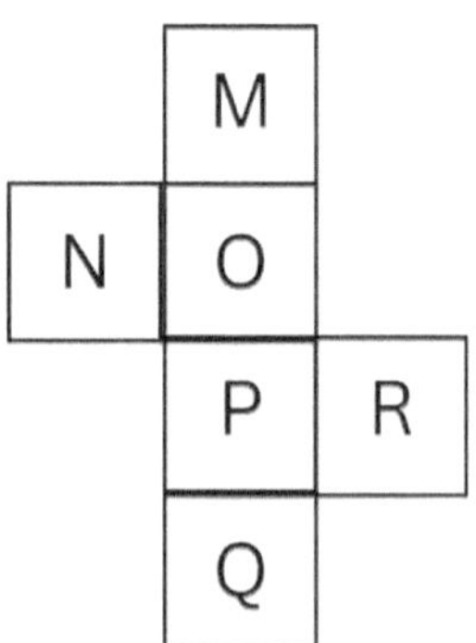

a. N, O; P, R; M, Q

b. N, P; O, R; M, Q

c. N, M; O, P; Q, R

d. N, R; M, P; O, Q

5.

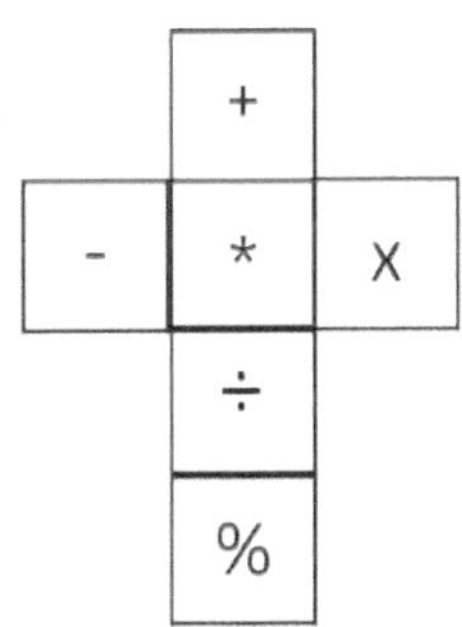

a. +, ÷; -, ×; *, %

b. +, *; ÷, %; -, x

c. +, *; -, ÷; ×, %

d. -, +; *, %; x, ÷

6.

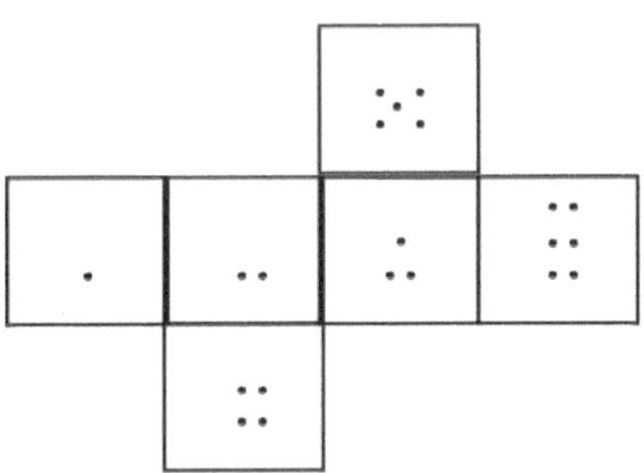

a

b

c

d

7.

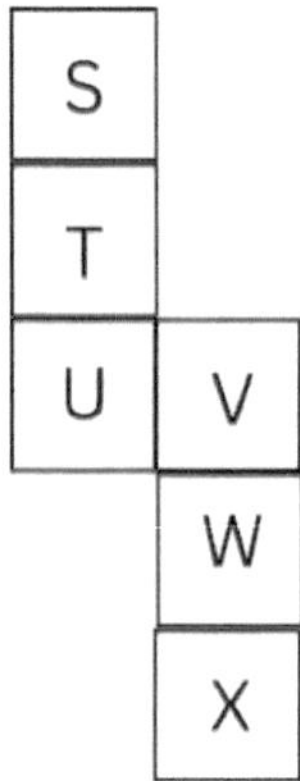

a. T, V; U, W; S, X

b. S, T; U, V; W, X

c. S, W; T, X; U, V

d. S, U; T, W; V, X

8.

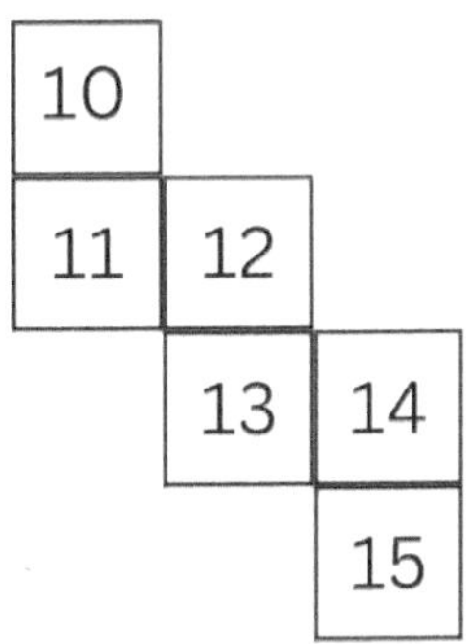

a. 10, 11; 12, 13; 14, 15

b. 10, 12; 11, 13; 14, 15

c. 11, 12; 10, 13; 14, 15

d. 10, 13; 11, 14; 12, 15

9.

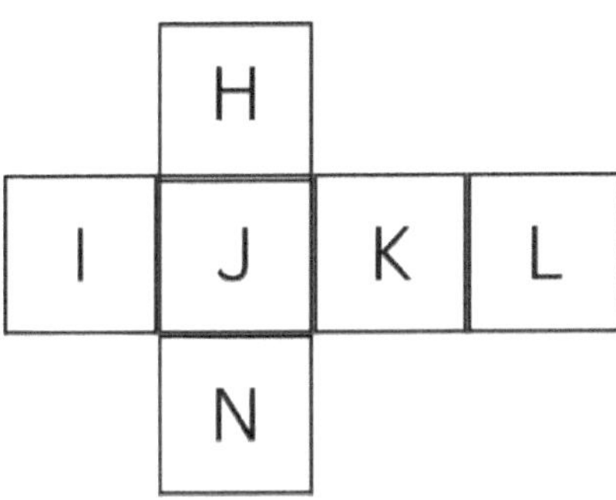

a. I, J; K, L; M, N

b. I, K; J, L; M, N

c. I, M; J, N; K, L

d. I, L; M, N; J, K

10.

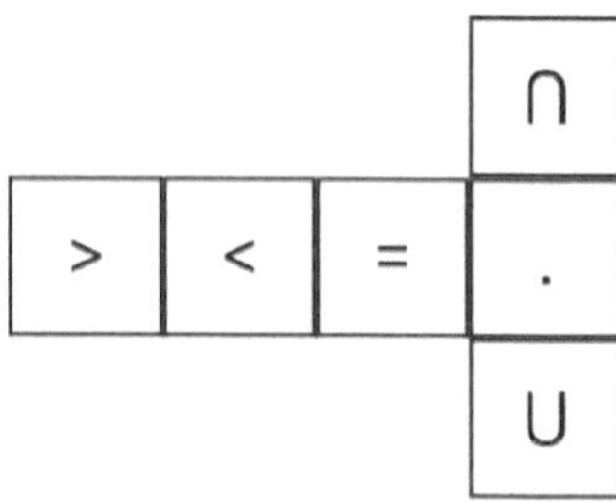

(a) >, = ; <, • ; ∩,U
(b) >, < ; =, • ; ∩,U
(c) >, < ; =,∩ ; • ,U
(d) >, • ; <,∩; =,U

11.

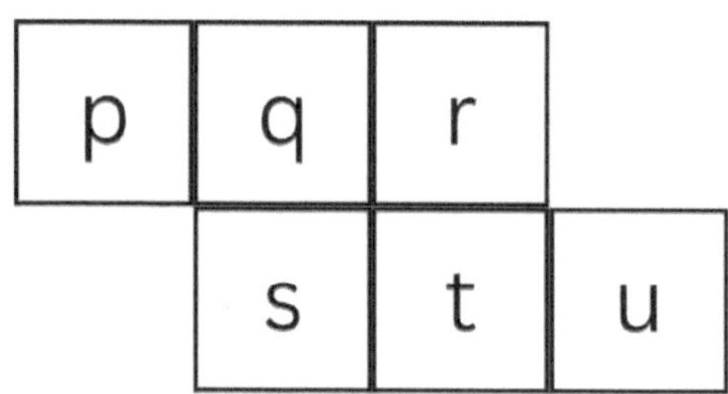

a. P, Q; R, S; T, U

b. P, U; Q, T; R, S

c. P, R; Q, T; S; U

d. P, T; Q, U; R, S

CHAPTER 10

DIRECTIONAL TESTS

Introduction

This chapter has problems involving directions, there are four main directions N- North, E-East, W-West, S-South and four secondary directions NE-North east, NW-North west, SE-South east, SW-Southwest.

What if person moving in a certain direction takes a left or right? Let' see

Direction, person is moving	**Direction of person who**	**Is taking a turn**
	Right turn	**Left turn**
North	East	West
South	West	East
East	South	North
West	North	South

The turn is 90° here, the short cutline from start to end is dotted.

If in a statement there is one way route from X to Y

X---------->Y I show it is represented

If in a statement, there is 2 way route from X to Y

X <--------->Y Is how it is represented

Worked Examples

1) Ray walked 1km West from his home, took a right turn, walked 2km after that, he then turned left and walked 3km&took a left turn and walked 5km, how far is he from his home

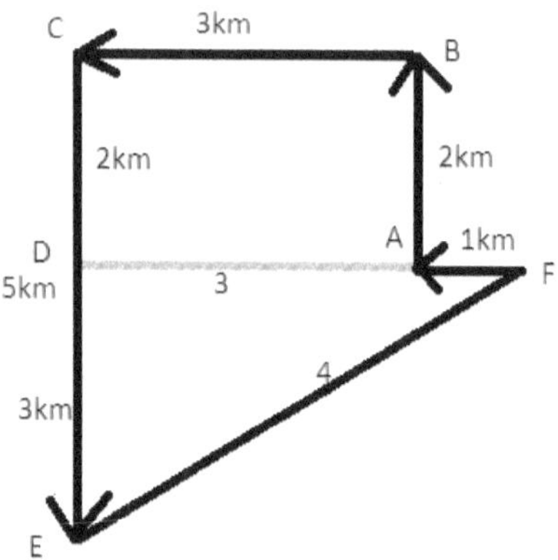

1) The figure is shown, so if we consider FDE as a right triangle:

$FD^2 + DE^2 = EF^2$

$(FA + AD)^2 + DE^2 = EF^2$

$(1 + 3)^2 + 3^2 = EF^2$

$EF^2 = 25$

$EF = 5$

Therefore, Ray is 5 km away from his home.

2) Four people A, B, C, & D are stationed in four corners of a square plot. A & B move 1½ sides clockwise & C and D move 1½ side anti-clockwise.

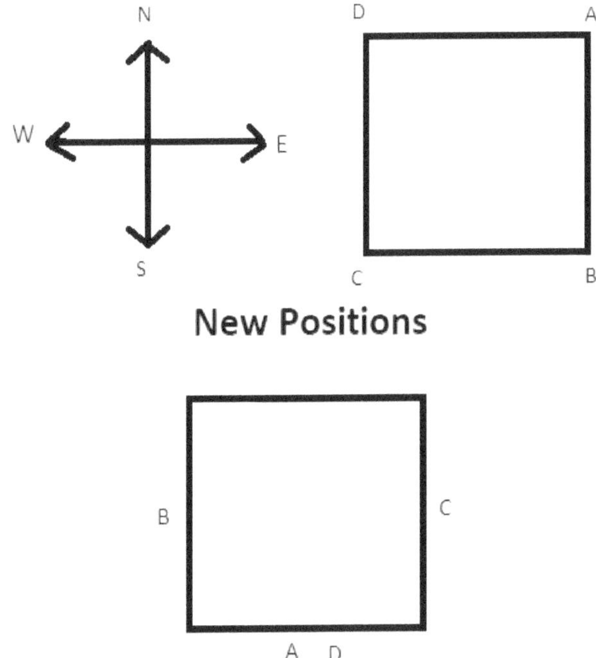

a) Who are the two people who are at the same place?

1. A & B
2. B & C
3. A & D
4. B & D

ANS: c. A and D

b) What direction is C to D?

1. NW
2. SW
3. SE
4. NE

ANS: d. NE

c) If A moves ½ side more clockwise, which of the following is the order of four people?

1. BADC
2. BDCA
3. CABD
4. CADB

ANS: a. BADC

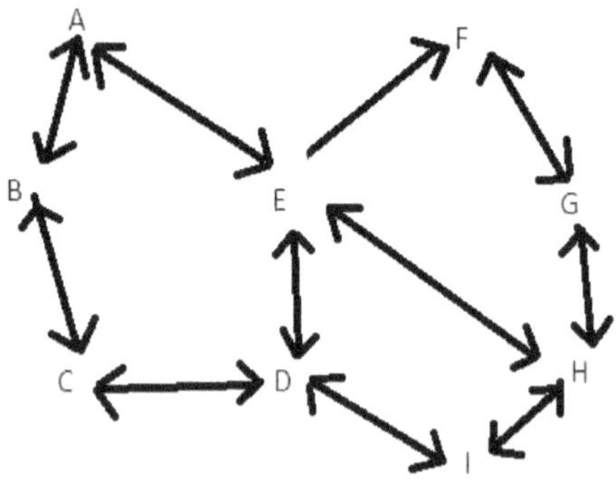

3. A, B, C, D, E, F, G, H, I are 9 places on a map. The following places are connected by 2-way roads: A&B, B&C, C&D,

D&E, E&A, D&I, F&G, G&H, H&I, I&D, E&H. Only E to F is one way, no other roads exist.

1. How many distinct routes exist from A to G?

a. 1

b. 2

c. 3

d. 6

2. Which is the shortest route from B to G?

a. B-C-D-E-H-G

b. B-C-D-I-H-G

c. B-A-E-F-G

d. B-A-E-D-I-H-G

ANS: c) B-A-E-F-G

3. The route covering the maximum number of places from C to H does not pass through:

a. E

b. I

c. F

d. B

Answer Explanation

1)The different routes from A to Gare

1. A-E-F-G
2. A-E-H-G
3. A-B-C-D-I-H-G
4. A-B-C-D-E-H-G,
5. A-B-C-D-E-F-G
6. A-E-D-I-H-G, So answer is 4

3. The route is C-B-A-E-F-G-H, It does not pass through I.

Exercise

1. Ram walks 3 km south, then he turns right, walks 4 km, again he turns right & walks 3 km. How far is he from the starting point?

2. Shubha traveled 10 km west starting from point A, then she turns left and moves 15 km, then she moves right and moves 5 km. She then turns right and goes 20 km, then turns right and moves 15 km. How far is she from the starting point?

3. Ravi traveled 10 km north, then turned right and walked 6 km, then he turned right and walked 2 km. How far is he from the starting point?

4. Kedar moved 5 km north, then turned left to walk 10 km, and then again turned left and moved 12 km, turns left to

walk 4 km, again left and moves 7 km. How far is he from where he started?

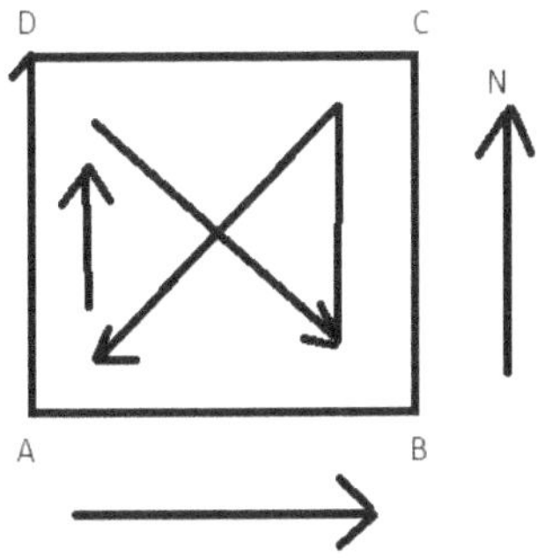

5. In the given figure, A, B, C, and D are 4 people at 4 corners of a plot. C and D move to opposite corners diagonally & move one side each clockwise and anti-clockwise respectively. B and A move one side clockwise and anti-clockwise respectively.

a) What is the new position of B?

a. NW corner

b. NE corner

c. SW corner

d. SE corner

b) What is the new position of D?

a. NW corner

b. NE corner

c. SW corner

d. SE corner

6. There are four people stationed at 4 corners of a square plot. A moves diagonally half the distance, turns left, walks a little bit, and again turns left. Which direction is A facing now?

a. NE

b. NW

c. SE

d. SW

7. From the position of A, B, C, and D at the corners of the plot, A and B move anti-clockwise one side and move diagonally to the opposite side, C and D move anti-clockwise one side.

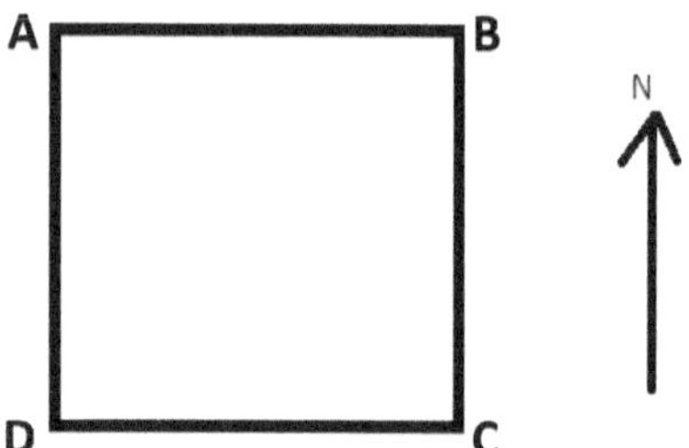

a) Which of the following is not an arrangement?

a. BCDA

b. ADCB

c. ACBD

d. ABCD

b) Where is B now located?

a. NE corner

b. NW corner

c. SE corner

d. SW corner

8. Mrs. Niru started from her house, she went 2 km north, then turned left and went 1 km, from there she turned left and went 4 km, then she turned right and covered 1 km. At the end, she turned right and covered 2 km to reach the hospital. How far is her house from the hospital?

a. 2 km

b. 4 km

c. 3 km

d. 5 km

9. If I stand facing east, in which direction will my left hand point?

a. South

b. North

c. Southeast

d. Northwest

10. A person is facing west, he turns 45° clockwise and then 180° anti-clockwise and 135° in the same direction. Which direction is he facing now?

a. South

b. East

c. North

d. West

11. A and B start from the same point but move off in opposite directions. A moves 1 km west, turns right, moves 2 km, and stops there. B moves 1 km east and turns right, moves 1 km, turns left, and moves 2 km, turns left again, and moves 3 km. What is the distance between A and B?

a. 2 km

b. 3 km

c. 4 km

d. 5 km

12. Two cars start from opposite points of the main road, 120 km apart. A moves 10 km towards east towards B, turns right, moves 20 km, turns left, moves 30 km, turns left and moves 20 km. B moves on the main road towards A for 50 km. What is the distance between A and B?

a. 10 km

b. 20 km

c. 30 km

d. 40 km

13. A woman turns left towards her left at right angles, next she again turns left, 3rd time she turns at right angles towards left and faces west. Which direction was she facing at the beginning?

a. South

b. East

c. North

d. West

14. A clock is placed in such a way that its hands point towards the southwest direction at 12:00 noon. In which direction does the hour hand point at 3:00 PM?

a. NE

b. NW

c. SW

d. SE

15. 4 people A, B, C, and D are standing on a circular path as shown:

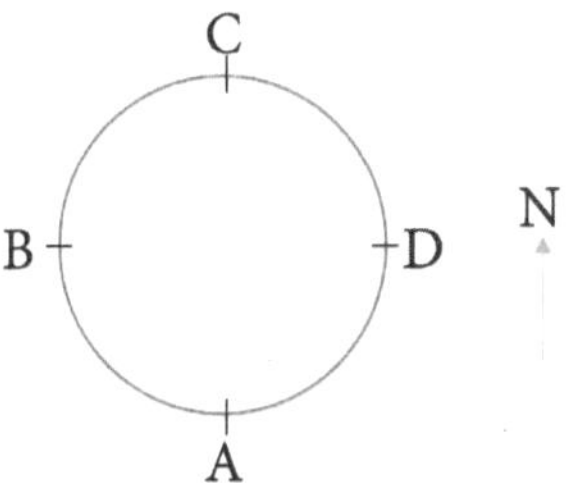

A moves ¼th of a turn clockwise, D moves ¼th of a turn anti-clockwise, if E stands exactly in the middle of A and D's new position on the circle, which direction is E facing?

a. NW
b. NE
c. SW
d. SE

16. From earlier position of A and C moved to opposite corner diametrically and moved ¼ Circle anticlockwise and clockwise respectively. Angle between A and C 's new position is:

a. 90 degree
b. 0 degree
c. 180 degree
d. 270 degree

17. From earlier positions, B and D move clockwise by π radians. Which direction is D now in?

a. South
b. East
c. North
d. West

18. From earlier positions, A and B move clockwise 45° and C and D move anti-clockwise by 90°. Which is the clockwise new arrangement?

a. ACBD

b. DBCA

c. ABCD

d. DCBA

LANDMARKS: A, B, C, D, E, F, G, and H

- B is 1 km west of A
- C is 3 km east of A
- G is 2 km south of A
- D is 2 km north of C
- E is 3 km west of D
- F is 1 km south of E
- H is 3 km east of G

19. Which 4 are in a straight line?

a. BAGH

b. BACD

c. DCHG

d. EFAG

20) How far is F from G and in which direction?

a. 3 km North

b. 3 km East

c. 3 km West

d. 2 km North

CHAPTER 11

CONSTRUCTION OF SQUARES AND TRIANGLES

In this chapter, the problems will be of the following type: You will be given 5 different shapes. You will be asked to put any 3 of them together to get a square or a triangle as the case may be.

Example 1: 3 out of 5 alternative figures will fit to form a square. Find the 3 figures.

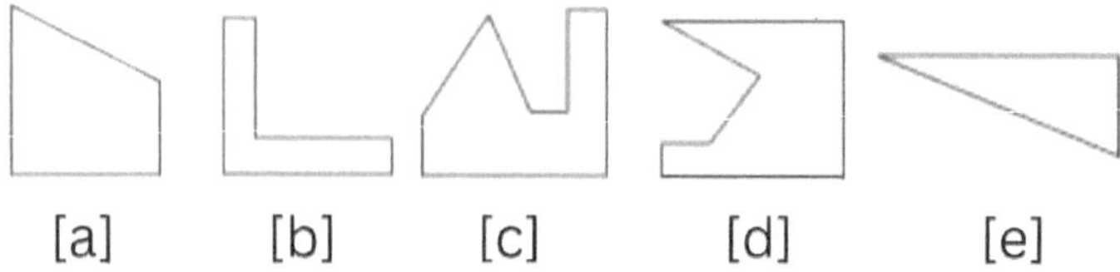

a, c and e fit this way:

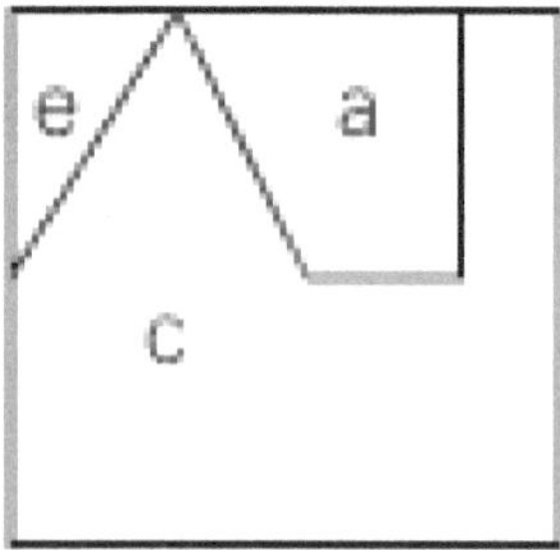

(Here, there is an illustration showing how the shapes fit together.)

Example 2: 3 out of 5 alternative figures will fit to form a triangle. Find the 3 figures.

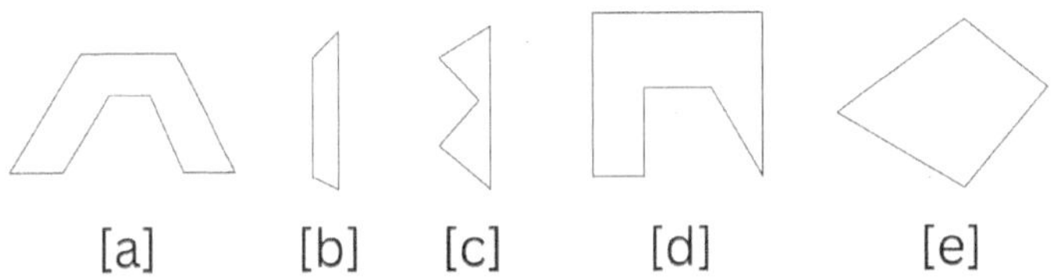

These 3 fit in the following way:

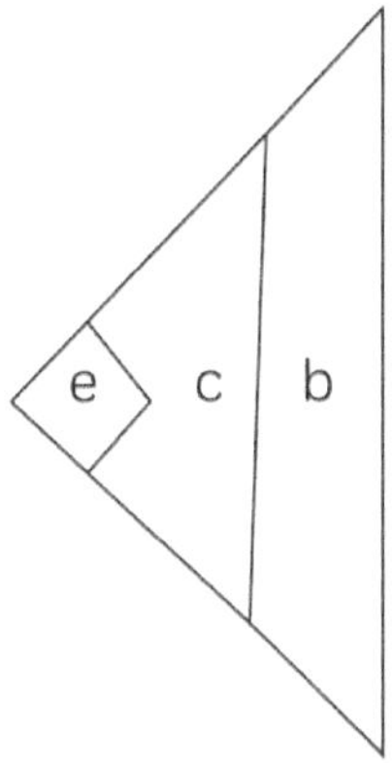

Exercise - 3 out of 5 alternatives will fit to form a square. Find the 3 figures.

1.

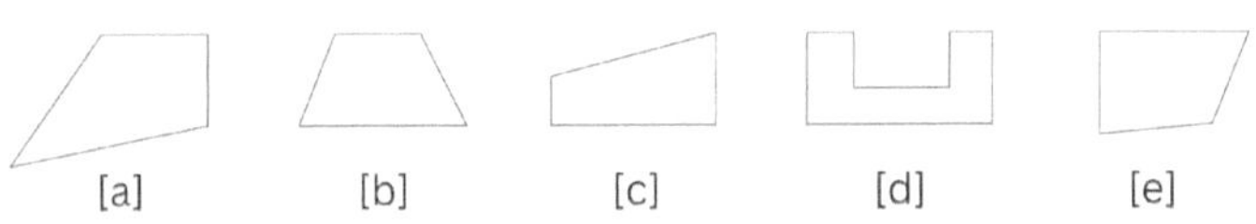

2.

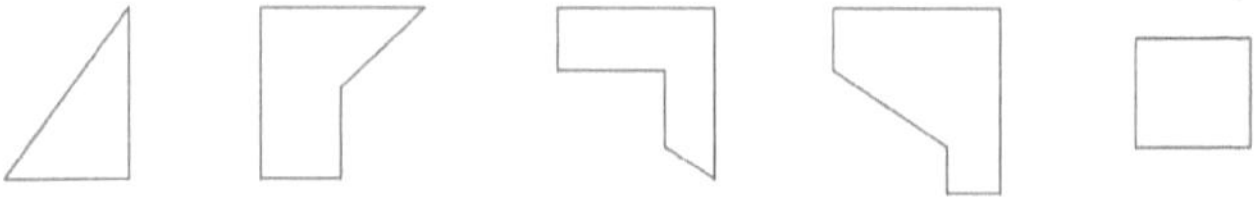

[a] [b] [c] [d] [e]

3.

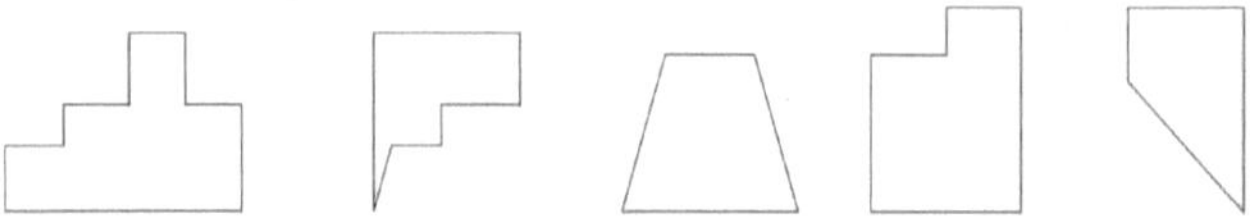

[a] [b] [c] [d] [e]

4.

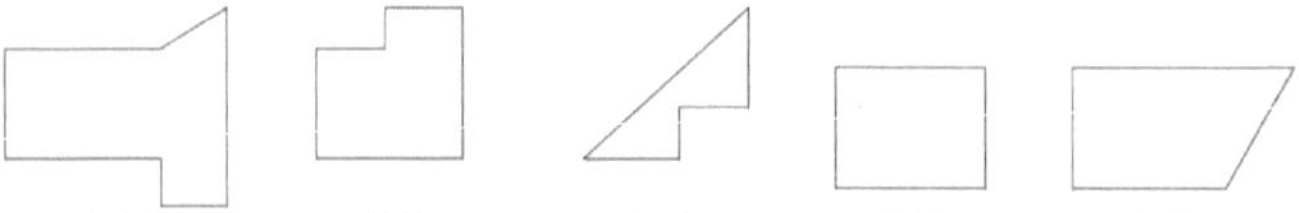

[a] [b] [c] [d] [e]

5.

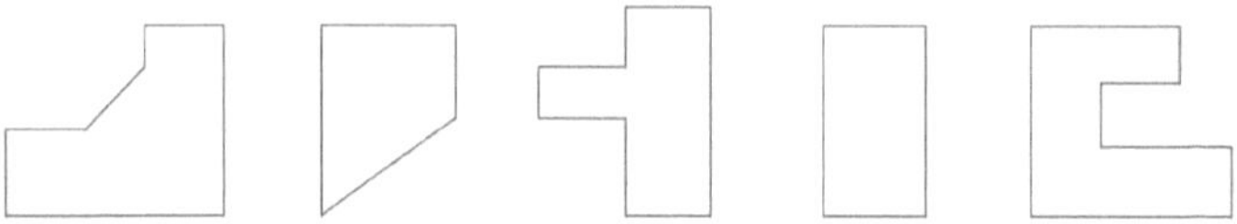

[a] [b] [c] [d] [e]

6.

[a] [b] [c] [d] [e]

7.

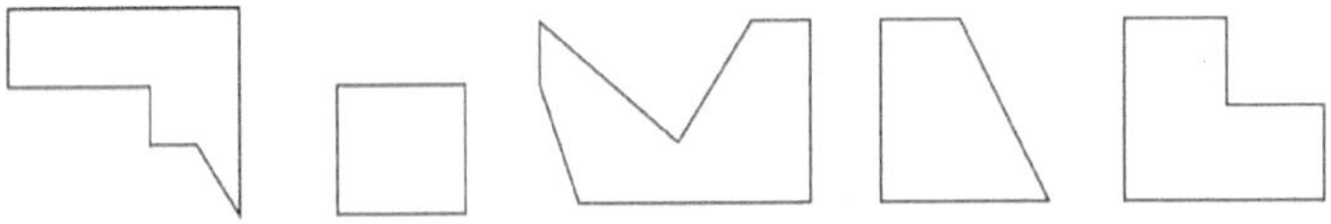

[a] [b] [c] [d] [e]

8.

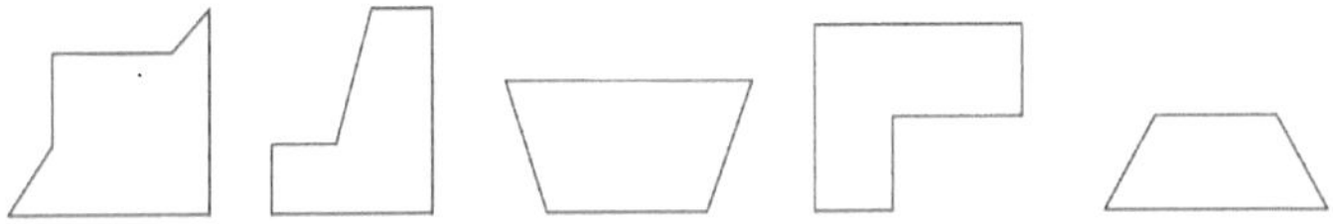

[a] [b] [c] [d] [e]

9.

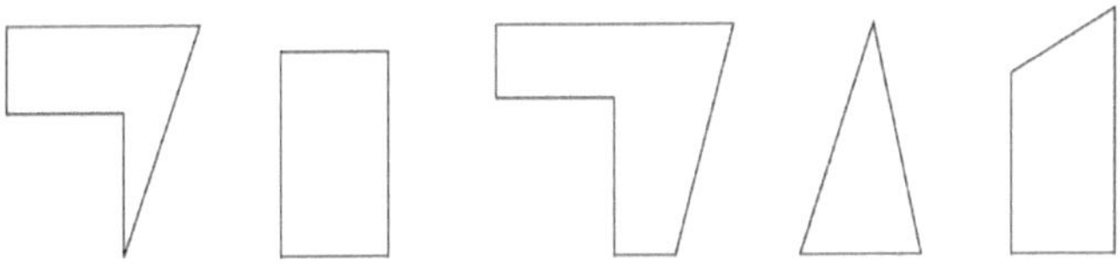

[a] [b] [c] [d] [e]

10.

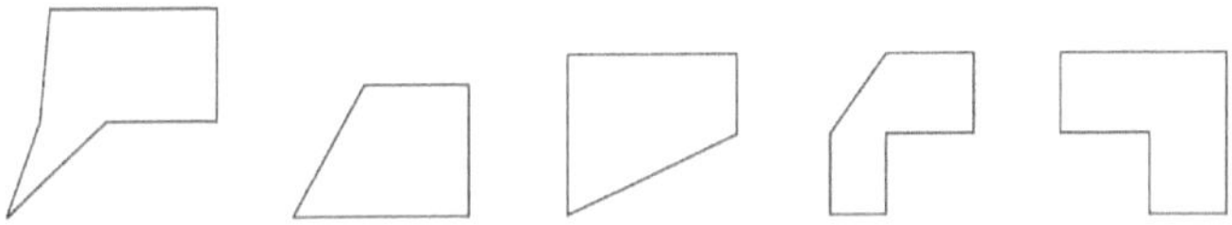

[a] [b] [c] [d] [e]

11.

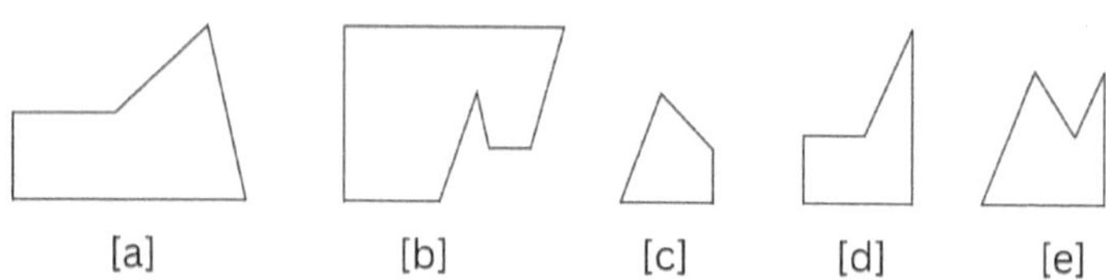

12.

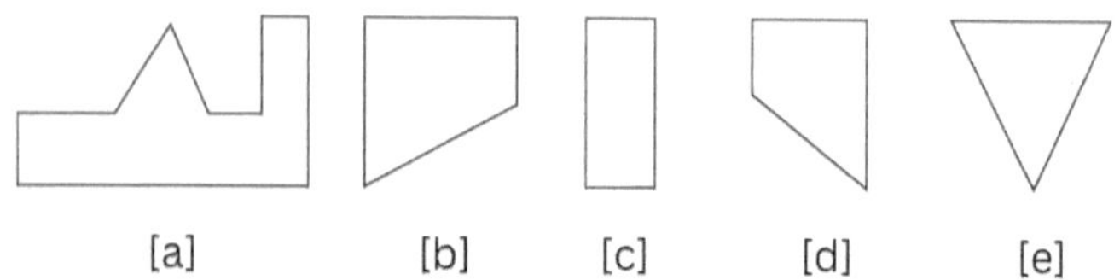

13.

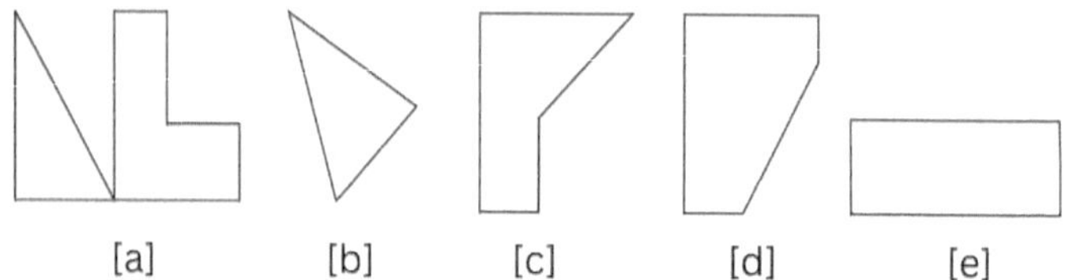

14.

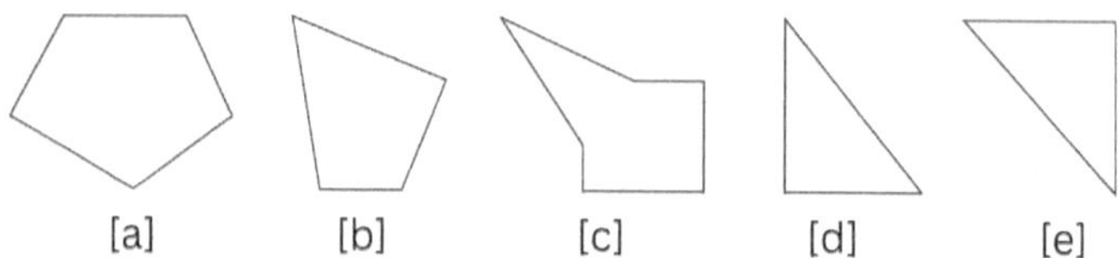

3 out of 5 alternatives will fit to form a triangle. Find the 3 figures.

15.

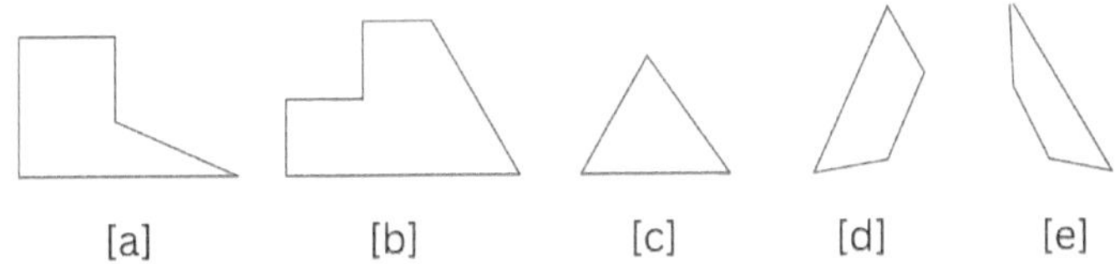

16.

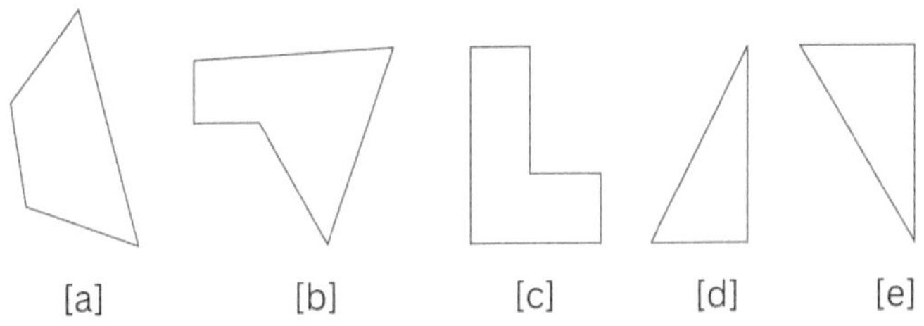

17.

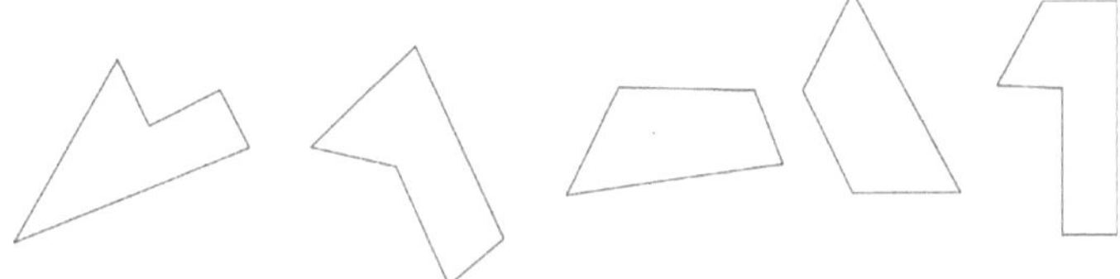

CHAPTER 12

BRAIN TEASERS

1. There are some hens and some rabbits in a poultry farm. There are 79 heads and 266 legs seen. How many rabbits are there

2. There are 7 badminton players. If each player plays with another only once, how many matches are played?

3. Raj's present age is 7 times his son's age. After 10 years, Raj's age will be 3 times his son's age. What are their present ages?

4. Sum of the 2 digits of a number is 13. If 45 is added to the number, the digits gets reversed. What is the 2 digit number?

5. An amoeba gives rise to 2 daughter cells 1st day. Each of the daughter amoebas give rise to 2 new daughter amoebas the 2nd day. Thus if on 1st day, there are 2 amoebas, the 2nd day, there are 4 amoebas, the 3rd day, there are 8 and so on. On which day are there 256 amoebas.

6. A fraction becomes equal to 1 if 1 is added only to numerator and becomes equal to ½ if 2 is added only to denominator. Find the initial fraction

7. The number of autorickshaws is 4 times the number of cycles in a town. The number of taxis is 5 times the number of autos. The number of buses is 6 times the number of taxis.

If number of buses is 1200, how many cycles are there in the town

8. If 5 pens and 3 pencils cost Rs41, and 8 pens and 1 pencil costs Rs 58, what is cost of 1 pen and 1 pencil

9. Three water color paintings are worth 12 mandala paintings. 9 mandalas are worth 21 lippan paintings. 27 lippan paintings are worth 6 tanjore paintings. If 2 tanjore paintings cost 75,600, what is cost of one water color painting?

10. A wire is bent in the form of an equilateral triangle with side 8 cm. It is then straightened and bent into the form of a square. What will be the side of square?

11. Two trains, Xand Y leave station A at same time and reach station B. The distance between stations is 400km. Train X reaches B in 5 hours and train Y travels at speeds 20km/hr more than speed of train X. How much time is taken by train Y to reach B.

12. A bottle is filled with juice. One third of that juice with bottle weighs 380gms. If empty bottle weighs 170gms, how much will the bottle filled with juice weigh?

13. A monkey eats 1 banana 1st day, 3 bananas 2nd day, 5 bananas 3rd day and so on.How many bananas would it have totally eaten from day 1 to day 15

14. If at a certain time of day, a tower 30m tall is making a shadow of 5m, how tall will the flagpost be to make a shadow of 3m at same time

15. If the length of rectangle increases by 2 and breadth decreases by 2, then the area decreases by 16. The same thing happens when length is decreased by 4 and breadth increased by 2. What is the original length and breadth.

16. In a set of 211 fruits, there are 6 less guavas than apples. There are 7 more oranges than apples. How many guavas are there

17. A vegetable seller sells 50% of the vegetables. 10% are rotten and thrown away. Out of remaining, 60% are sold the next day and remaining are rotten and thrown away. What % of the vegetables are rotten and thrown away

18. Mr Raj distributed equal number of chocolates he bought from U>S to his 5 cousins and had 2 cholotates left. He took another pack containing same number of chocolates and distributed equal number of them to 7 uncles and has 2 left. He took another pack with same number of chocolates and gave them to 6 aunts and had 2 chocolates left. What is the least number of chocolates that the pack contained.

19. In a pack of playing cards, what is the probability that a person randomly picks a black king?

20. In a shooting competition, a marksman receives 50 paise if he hits the mark and pays 20 paise if he misses it. He tried 60 shots and was paid Rs 1.30. How many times did he hit the mark

21. A 2 digit number is such that the ten's digit exceeds twice the units digit by 2 and the number obtained by

interchanging the digits is 5 more than 3 times the sum of the digits. Find the 2 digit number

22. Ajit says to Ram, “Give me a hundred, I shall then become twice as rich as you”. Ram replies, if you give me ten, I shall be 6 times as rich as you.” How much does each have originally?

23. A and B are friends and A is older than B by 2 years. A’s father D is twice as old as A and B is twice as old as his sister C. The ages of D and C differ by 40 years. Find the ages of A and B

SOLUTIONS

LETTER AND WORD ANALOGY

1.

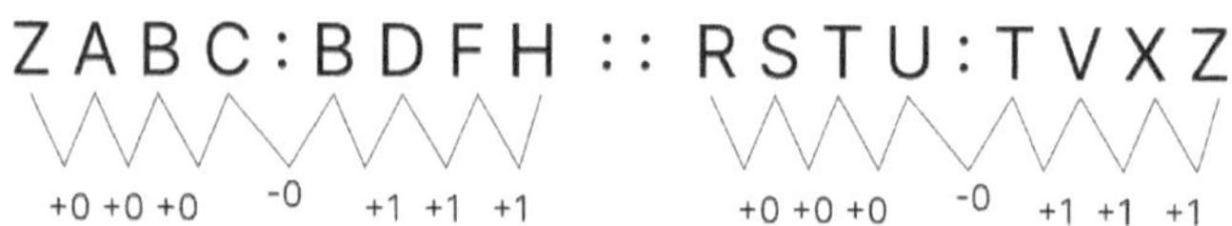

Ans (c) RSTU

2.

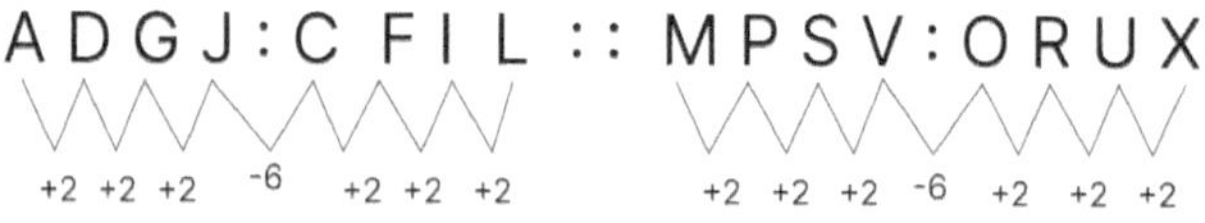

Ans (a) CFIL

3.

ACEG : YWUS :: EGIK : USQO

+1 +1 +1 -1 -1 -1 +1 +1 +1 -1 -1 -1

Ans (a) USQO

4.

BACED : FEGIH :: LKMON : POQSR

-0 +1 +1 -0 +1 -0 +1 +1 -0 -0 +1 +1 -0 +1 -0 +1 +1 -0

Ans (a) POQSR

5.

M J G D : N Q T W :: O L I F : P S V Y

-2 -2 -2 +9 +2 +2 +2   -2 -2 -2 +9 +2 +2 +2

Ans (b) OLIF

6.

B X D V : Y C W E :: F T H R : U G S I

X is before Y, which is a corresponding letter of B.

V is before W, which is a corresponding letter of D.

Y corresponds to B, C to X, W to D, and E to V.

T is before U, which is a corresponding letter of F.

R is before S, which is a corresponding letter of H.

U corresponds to F, G to T, S to H, and I to R.

Ans (d) UGSI

7.

A D H N : P S W C :: G F J P : R U Y E

+2 +3 +5 +1 +2 +3 +5   +2 +3 +5 +1 +2 +3 +5

Ans (c) PSWC

8.

Z W T Q : B E H K :: Y V S P : A D G J

-2 -2 -2 +10 +2 +2 +2   -2 -2 -2 +10 +2 +2 +2

Ans (a) BEHK

9.

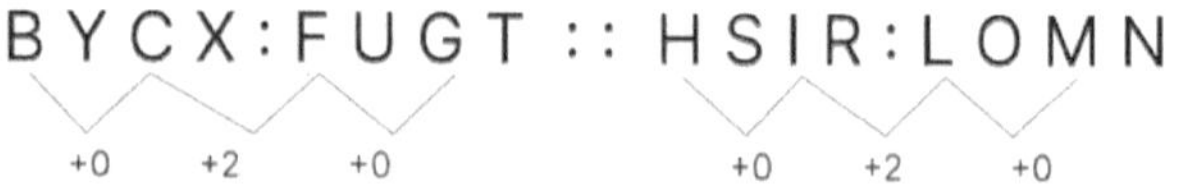

B corresponds to Y & C corresponds to X

F corresponds to U & G corresponds to T

H corresponds to S & I corresponds to R

L corresponds to O & M corresponds to N

Ans (d) LOMN

10.

ABCD:XWVU :: CDEF:VUTS

+0 +0 +0 -0 -0 -0 +0 +0 +0 -0 -0 -0

A corresponds to Z & ZX is -1

C corresponds to X & XV is -1

Ans (c) CDEF

11.

YVSP:MJGD :: AXUR:OLIF

-2 -2 -2 -2 -2 -2 -2 -2 -2 -2 -2 -2 -2 -2

Ans (b) MJGD

12.

X V T R : Y A C E :: S Q O M : T V X Z

-1 -1 -1 +1 +1 +1 -1 -1 -1 +1 +1 +1

Ans (b) TVXZ

13. Impediment means hindrance and impending means nearing

Sol: (b) nearing

14. Mortician means undertaker, similarly mortify means to humiliate

Sol: (d) Humiliate

15. Occlude means to shut. Similarly odious means hateful

Sol: (a) Odious

16. Just as tailor works with sewing machine, a woodcutter works with axe

Sol: (d) Axe

17. just as printer is an output device, keyboard is an input device

Sol: (d) keyboard

18. Rancor and love are opposites just as recipient and giver are opposites

Sol: ©love

19. Severance means separation. Similarly severity means harshness

Sol: (d) Harshness

20. Thrive means flourish.Throttle means strangle

Sol: (a) Throttle

21. Wzardry means sorcery. Wily means cunning

Sol: (a) Wily

22.Just as animosity means active enmity, annihilate means to destroy

Sol: (a) Annihilate

23. Dilate means enlarge which is opposite of contract. Dilemma means problem whose opposite is solution

Sol: (b) Solution

24. Table is made of wood. Aeroplane is made of aluminium

Sol: © Aeroplane

25. Fraudulent means cheating. Similarly fraught means filled with

Sol: (b) Filled

LETTER AND WORD ODDMAN

1. -3 is the difference between 1st to next letter for all (b),(c),(d),(e) except (a) ABEGI

Sol: (A)

2. +5,+4,+3,+2,+1 rule does not apply to © FILORW

Sol: (c)

3. +1,+2,+3,+4 rule does not apply to (b) EGIKM which is odd man out

Sol: (b)

4. -0,+4,-1,+5 rule applies to others except (c) AFCGE

Sol: (c)

5. +4,-6,+3,-5 rule applies for rest except (e)VZTXR

Sol: (e)

6. +8, -3,-3,+2 rule applies for all except (e) UZXVO

Sol: (e)

7. 1st,3rd and 5th letters are consecutive while 2nd, 4th and 6th are their corresponding letters. This rule is not followed by (b) GSIQLO

Sol: (b)

8. -2,+0,+2, -4 is rule followed by all except (c) IJHOG

Sol: (c)

9. Only (b) EFDIO has vowels in it

Sol: (b)

10. Decode all 5 words to get KERALA, CHENNAI, BOMBAY,MYSORE and LUCKNOW. Except KERALA, all others are cities.so (a) is odd one out

Sol: (a)

11. All other words have 2 vowels except NORTH, which has only 1 vowel

Sol: (e)

12. Except a) DGJNT, all others have prime numbered letters

Sol: (a)

13. I, K, M are not separated by 2 letters and their corresponding letters are not PRN. So (c) is odd one out.

Sol: (c)

Word odd man

14. Except "G.B.Shah", who is a writer, all others were scientists

Sol: (1)

15. All others, other than 'gas stove', are electronic gadgets.

Sol: (4)

16. Except 'play station', all others are musical instruments

Sol: (2)

17. Except 'Chotta bhim' others are girl comic character.

Sol: (1)

18. Except 'teacher' others are specialists in medicine

Sol: (4)

19. Except 'high jump', which is track and field event, all others are team sports.

Sol: (3)

20. Except 'pentagon', all others are quadrilaterals

Sol: (4)

21. Except 'Brisbane',all others are capitals of countries

Sol: (3)

22. Except 'paradise lost', all other books are written by Indians

Sol: (5)

23. Except "rectangle", all others are types of triangles

Sol: (2)

24. " Calligraphy", is not a type of painting while others are

Sol: (4)

25. Except "cardiology", all others are branches of engineering

Sol: (1)

26. Except "chlorine", which is non-metal, all others are metals

Sol: (3)

PYRAMID PUZZLES & NUMBER TRIANGLES

1. The pattern comes this way:

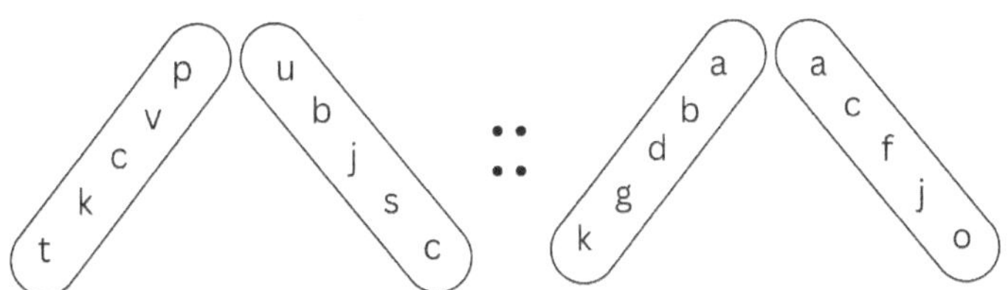

So the answer is (b) abdgk

---

2. The pattern comes this way:

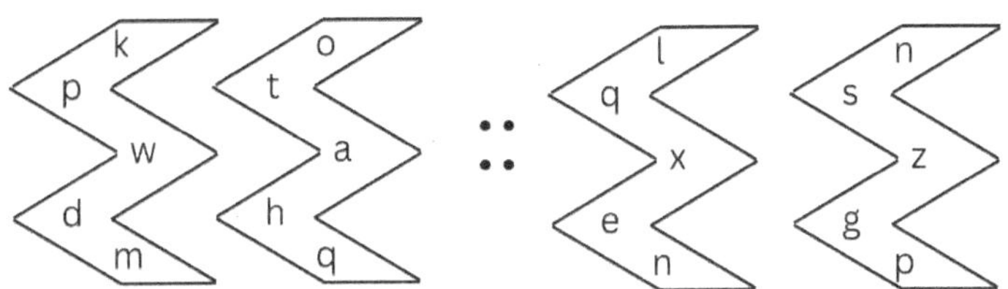

Ans (a) nszgp

---

3. The pattern comes this way:

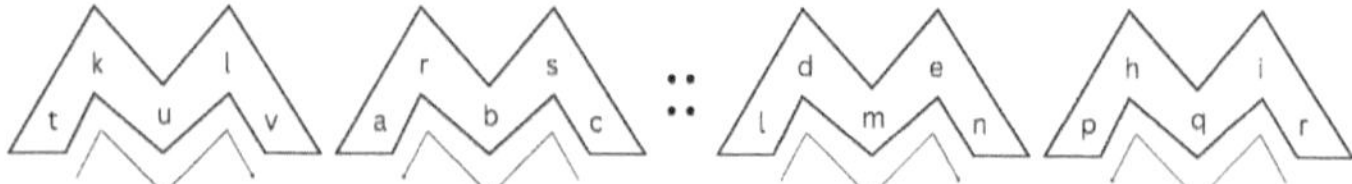

Ans (d) t k u l v

---

4. The pattern comes this way:

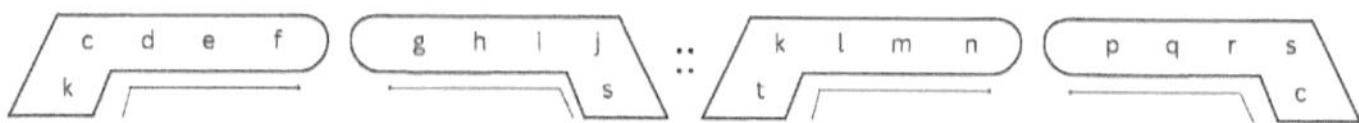

Ans (c) s j i h g

---

5. The pattern comes this way:

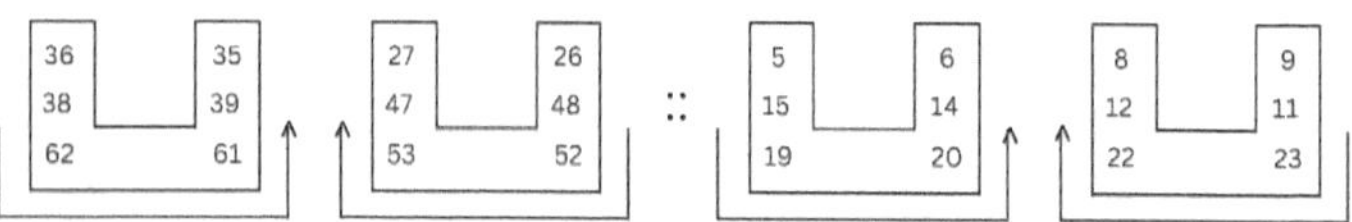

So the answer is (a) 9, 11, 23, 22, 12, 8

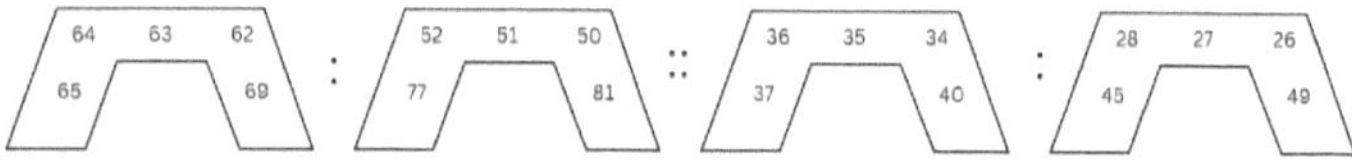

6. The pattern comes as above. So the answer is (b) 81, 50, 51, 52, 77

7.

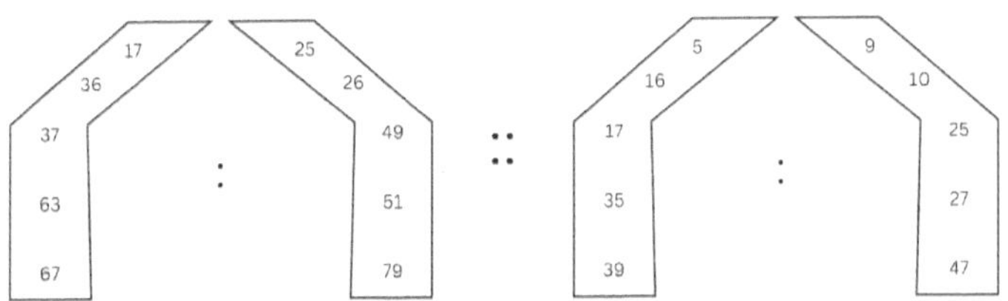

The pattern comes as above. So the answer is (d) 5, 16, 17, 35, 39

8.

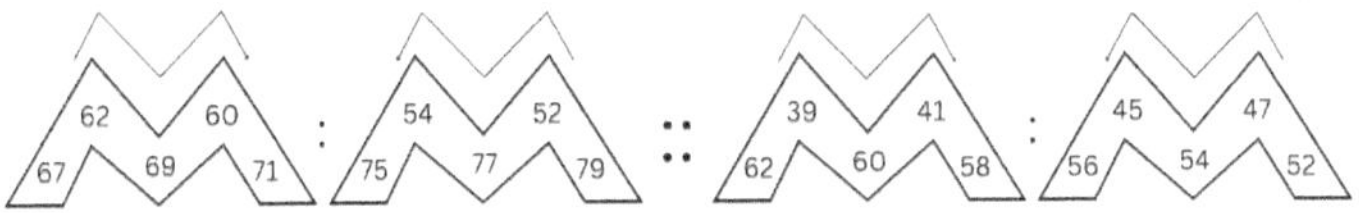

The pattern is as above. So the answer is (a) 52, 47, 54, 45, 56

9.

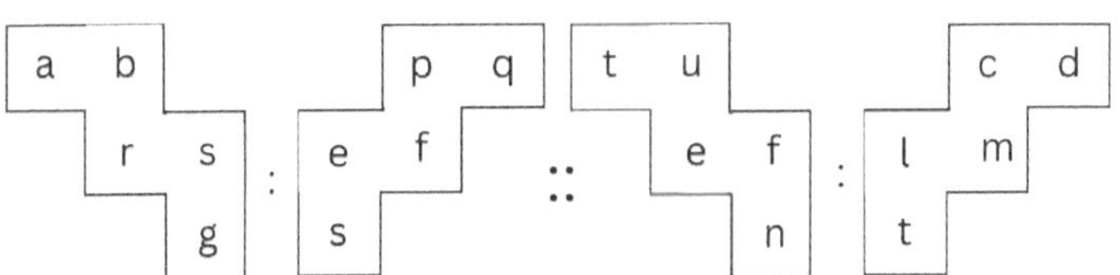

The pattern is as above..So the answer is (c) t u e f n

10.

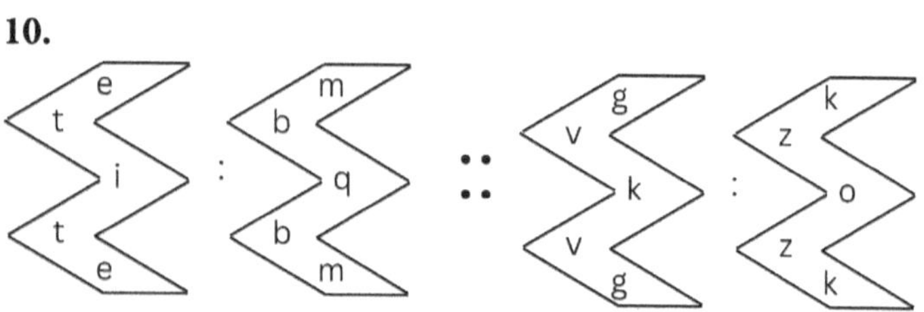

The pattern is as above. So the answer is (a) k z o z k

11.

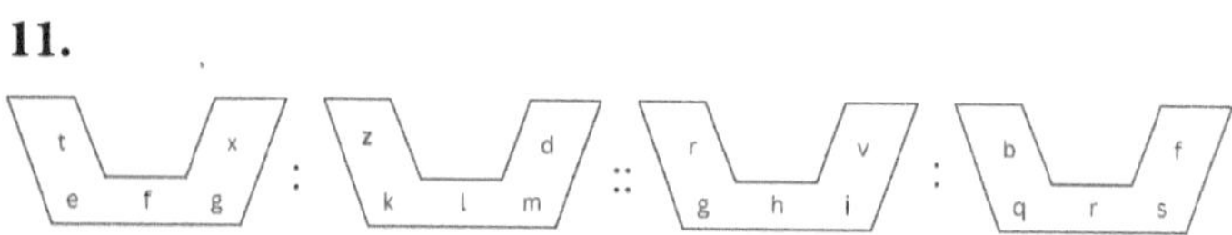

The pattern is as above. Answer is (a) d m l k z

12.

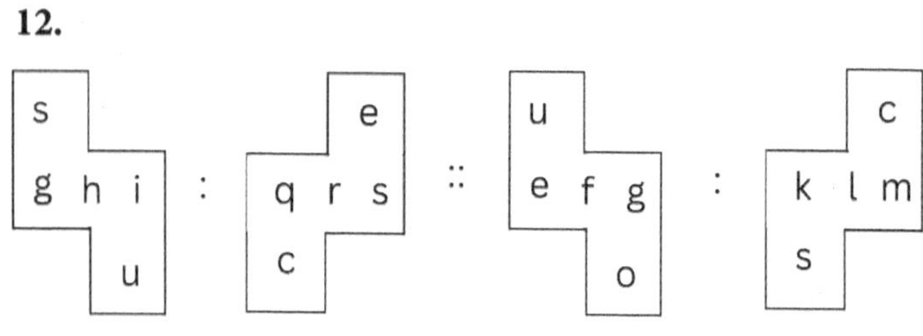

Pattern is as above. Answer is (a) u e f g o

13.

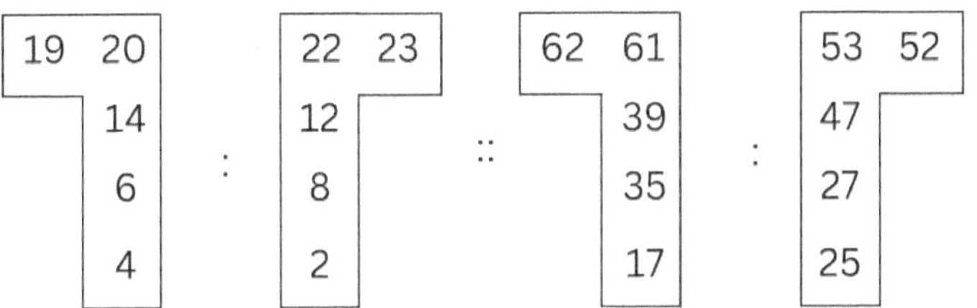

The pattern is as above. Answer is (b) 2, 8, 12, 22, 23

14.

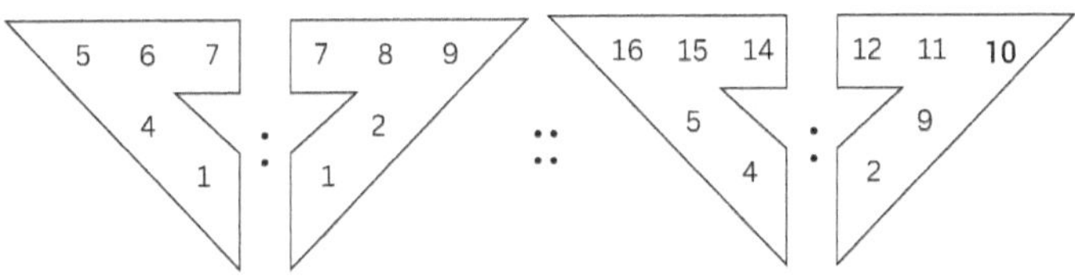

The pattern is as above. Answer is (d) 12, 11, 10, 9, 2

15.

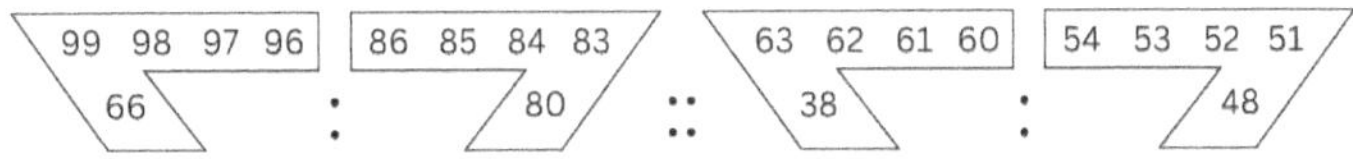

The pattern is as above. Answer is (a) 66, 99, 98, 97, 96

16.

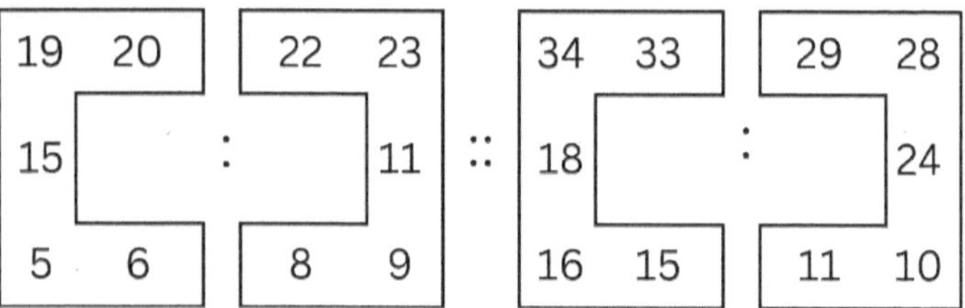

Pattern is as above. Answer is (b) 20, 19, 15, 5, 6

17.

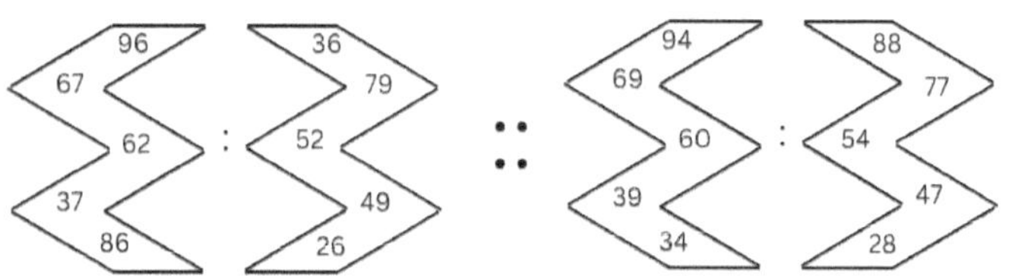

Pattern is as above. Answer is (a) 88, 77, 54, 47, 28

18.

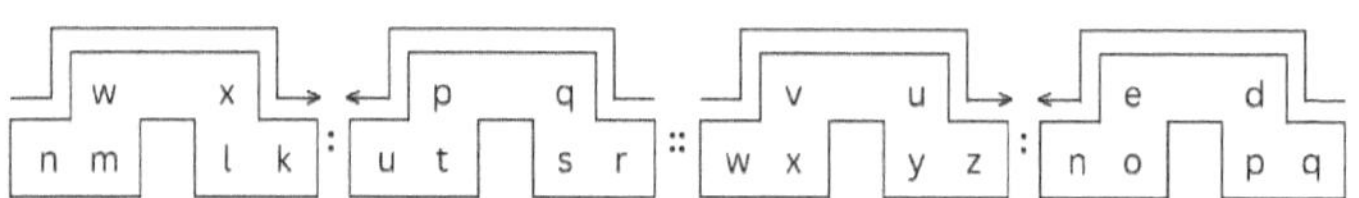

Pattern is as shown above. Answer is (c) r s q p t u

19.

Pattern is drawn as above. Answer is (a) l k j m h

20.

Pattern is as above. Answer is (d) s n g l w

21.

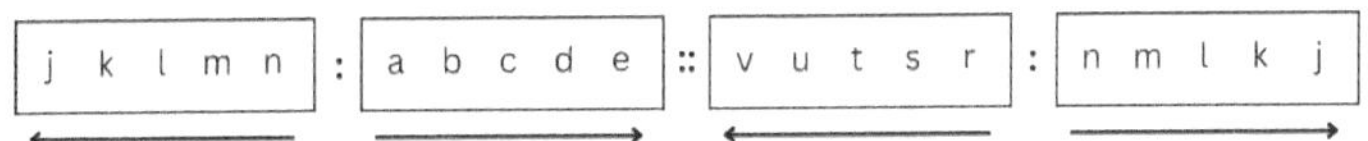

Pattern is as above. Answer is (b) r s t u v

CHAIN OF LETTERS AND NUMBERS

I. (1) one 2 is between 3 and 5, second 2 is between 1 and 7, third 2 is between 9 and 1, forth 2 is between 1 and 7, 5th is between 3 and 1. So totally 5, 2s are between 2 odd numbers

Sol (c) 5

2. Three 1s come before 2s.

Sol (b)3

3. 7 occurs 2 times. 2 occurs 8 times.So ratio is 2/8=1:4.

Sol (a) 1:4

4. 3 occurs 3 times, 2 occurs 8 times, 1 occurs 5 times, 5 occurs 1 time, 6 occurs 1 time, 7 occurs 2 times, 8 occurs 2 times, 9 occurs 1 time. From the options (c) 7 and 8 is correct as both occur 2 times.

5. If consecutive numbers are added, we get the following sums 6 5 7 6 2 3 9 9 8 14 16 10 11 11 3 3 9 8 4 5 3 3. So sum is 3 for 5 times.

Ans: (d) 5

II. The alphabets in English are L | m l k j I h g f e d c b a n o p q r s t u v w x y z | R

6. 17th letter from left is q and 16th letter from right is 'c'. There middle term is 'n'.

Ans: (c)n

7. 19 letters from right is 'f', from 'f', 4 letters to right is 'b'.

Sol: (a)b

8. 11th letter from left is 'c' and 20th from right is 'g'. In-between 'c' and 'g' are 3 letters.

Sol: (d) 3

9. on either side of 'n' are 'a' and 'o'.

Sol: (b) a and o

10. 13th letter from left is 'a'. To its right is 'n'.

Sol: (a)n

III. The alphabets are L | B A D C F E H G J I L K N M P O R Q T S V U X W Z Y | R

11. 15th letter from left is 'P' and 8th from right is 'T'. Middle of P and T is 'R'.

Sol: (d) R

12. 12th letter from left is 'k'. To its right is 'N'

Sol (b) N

13. 21st letter from left is 'v' 12th letter from right is 'T'. There are 5 letters in-between 'v' and 'T'.

Sol: (c) 5

14. 12th letter from right is 'P'.4th to right of P is 'T'. Sol: (b) T

15. On either side of L are I and K

IV. (16) Three 1s are followed by 6. Sol: (c) 3

17. First 1 is between 2 and 6, second 1 is between 2 and 4, third 1 is between 8 and 2, forth 1 is between 8 and 6. So totally, 4 ones between 2 even numbers.

18. 2 and 6 occurs 4 times. 1 occurs 5 times.2 occurs 4 times, 3 occurs 3 times, 4 occurs 1 time, 5 occurs 1 time, 6 occurs 4 times, 7 occurs 1 time, 8 occurs 2 times, 9 occurs 1 time Ans (a) 2 and 6

19. 8 occurs 2 times,6 occurs 4 times. Ratio is 2:4=1:2

Sol (d) 1:2

20. If consecutive numbers are added, the following sums are obtained 7 3 7 9 4 7 8 3 5 7 11 9 3 8 9 10 16 17 9 7 8. 7 occurs 5 times.

Sol: (d) 5

V. The alphabets are L| z x w v u t s r q p o n m l k j I h g f e d c b a y |R

21. 13th term from right is 'l'. 7th term to left of 'l' is 's'.

Sol (b) s

22. 11th term from right is 'j' and 'n' is 12th term from left. In between j and n are 3 terms

Sol: (c) 3

23. On right of 'a' is 'y'

Sol: (a) y

NUMBERS IN BRACKETS AND SQUARE CELLS

Type-1 -In all the problems from 1 – 15, name the 1st column as 'a', 2nd column as 'b', and 3rd column as 'c' and work out the rules accordingly.

1. b is obtained from 'a' and 'c' columns by the formula:

(a + c) / 2 squared (7 + 3) / 2 squared = 5^2 = 25

(4 + 2) / 2 squared = 3^2 = 9

(3 + 5) / 2 squared = 4^2 = 16

Answer = 16

2. a is obtained from 'b' and 'c' columns by the formula:

√(b * c) + 1

√(8 * 6) + 1 = 7

√(6 * 4) + 1 = 5

√(8 * 10) + 1 = 9

Answer = 5

3. c is obtained from 'a' and 'b' columns by the formula:

3a + b

3 * 3 + 4 = 13

3 * 2 + 5 = 11

$3 * 6 + 2 = 20$

Answer = 20

4. The formula used is:

$\sqrt{(a + c)} = b$

$\sqrt{(35 + 14)} = 7$

$\sqrt{(2 + 7)} = 3$

$\sqrt{(55 + 9)} = 8$

Answer = 8

5. The formula is a/3 + 2b

$12/3 + 2*4 = 12$

$18/3 + 2*3 = 12$

$21/3 + 2*2 = 11$

Answer = 12

6. Formula used is $a = \sqrt{b} - c$

$\sqrt{95} - 14 = 9$

$\sqrt{40} - 15 = 5$

$\sqrt{72} - 8 = 8$

Answer = 8

7. Formula is a + b^2 = c

12 + 4^2 = 28

6 + 5^2 = 31

$15 + 6^2 = 51$

Answer = 51

8. Formula is $a^2 - c^2 = b$

$6^2 - 3^2 = 27$

$12^2 - 11^2 = 23$

$10^2 - 8^2 = 36$

Answer = 36

9. Formula is $b^2 - \sqrt{c} = a$

$7^2 - \sqrt{81} = 49 - 9 = 40$

$9^2 - \sqrt{225} = 81 - 15 = 66$

$5^2 - \sqrt{169} = 25 - 13 = 12$

Answer = 66

10. Formula is $\sqrt{a} - 2c = b$

$\sqrt{100} - 2*3 = 4$

$\sqrt{81} - 2*4 = 1$

$\sqrt{196} - 2*2 = 10$

Answer = 10

11. Formula is $b^3 + c/2 = a$

$3^3 + 8/2 = 31$

$7^3 + 12/2 = 349$

$5^3 + 50/2 = 150$

Answer = 31

12. Formula used is $(\sqrt{a} * c) / 10=b$

$\sqrt{25} * 4 / 10 = 2$

$\sqrt{100} * 7 / 10 = 7$

$\sqrt{400} * 3 / 10 = 6$

Answer = 7

13. Formula is $\sqrt{a} + b / 2 = c$

$\sqrt{49} + 5 / 2 = 6$

$\sqrt{121} + 7 / 2 = 9$

$\sqrt{9} + 13 / 2 = 8$

Answer = 9

14. Formula is $\sqrt[3]{c} + b = a$

$\sqrt[3]{15} + 12 = 3$

$\sqrt[3]{195} + 21 = 6$

$\sqrt[3]{121} + 4 = 5$

Answer = 5

15. Formula b = a^2 - 3c

8^2 - 3*2 = 58

5^2-6*3=7

11^2 - 4*3 = 109

Answer = 109

Type-2

16. Write the missing number in number sequence that is 59

Write in increasing order

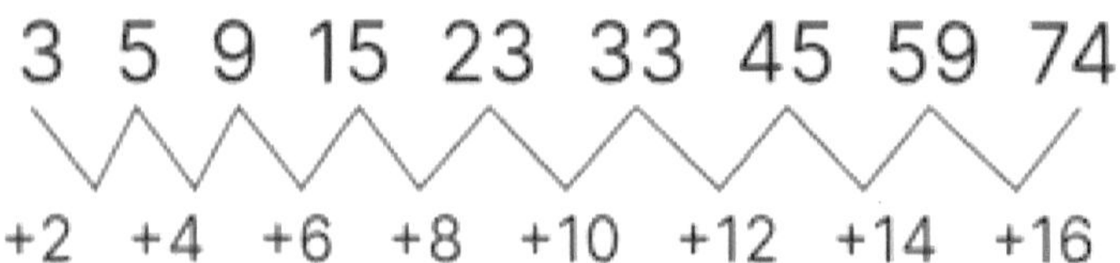

17. **Write the missing number in series that is 26**

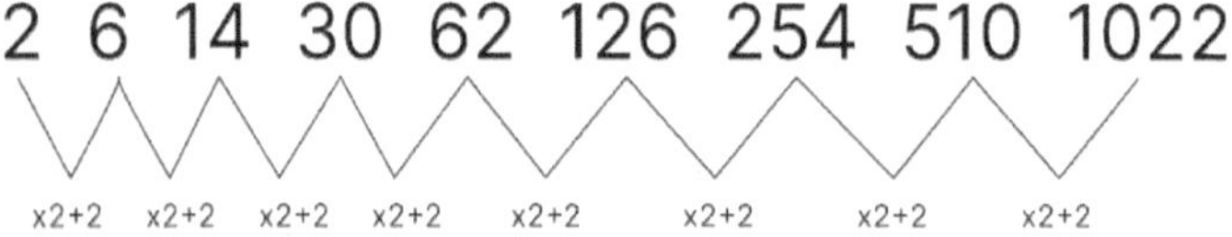

18. Write in increasing order & fill the blanks

2 6 14 30 62 126 254 510 1022

x2+2 x2+2 x2+2 x2+2 x2+2 x2+2 x2+2 x2+2

Write the missing number in the series that is 62

19. Write in increasing order & fill the blank

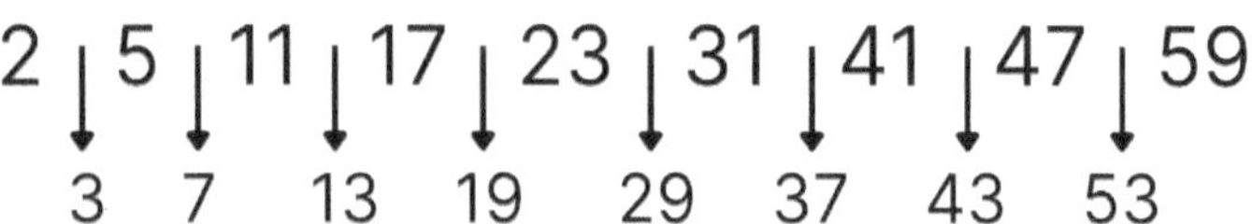

Write the missing number in series which is 11

20. Writing in increasing order

6	25	66	123	214	341	510	727	998
2^3-2	3^3-2	4^3-2	5^3-2	6^3-2	7^3-2	8^3-2	9^3-2	10^3-2

Write the missing number in series which is 510

21 Writing in increasing order

1 1 2 6 24 120 720 5040 40320

x1 x2 ×3 x4 x5 x6 x7 x8

Write the missing number that is 40320

22. ***Write in increasing order***

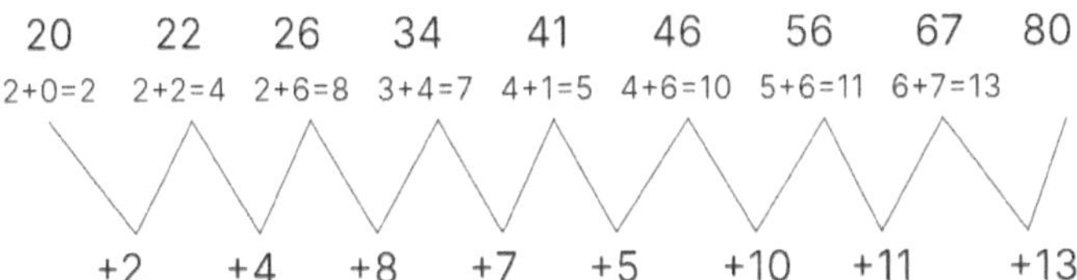

Write the missing number that is 41

23. The numbers are reversed

10	80	72	46	521	612	343	215	927
⟵	⟵	⟵	⟵	⟵	⟵	⟵	⟵	⟵
01	08	27	64	125	216	343	512	729
1^3	2^3	3^3	4^3	5^3	6^3	7^3	8^3	9^3

Write the missing term 343 in blank

24 Write in increasing order

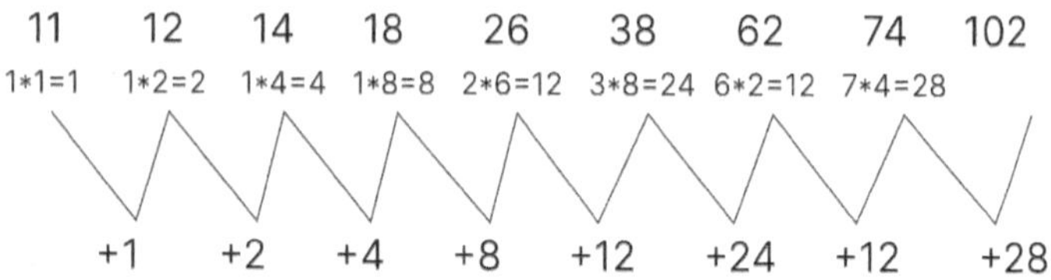

Write the missing term 14 in blank

25. Write in increasing order

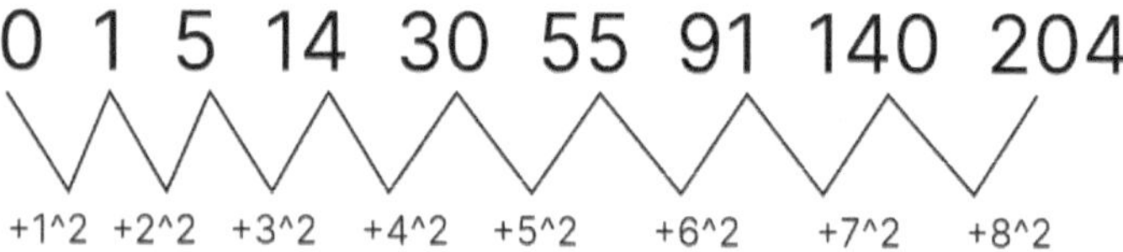

Write the missing term 14 in blank

26. ***Write in increasing order***

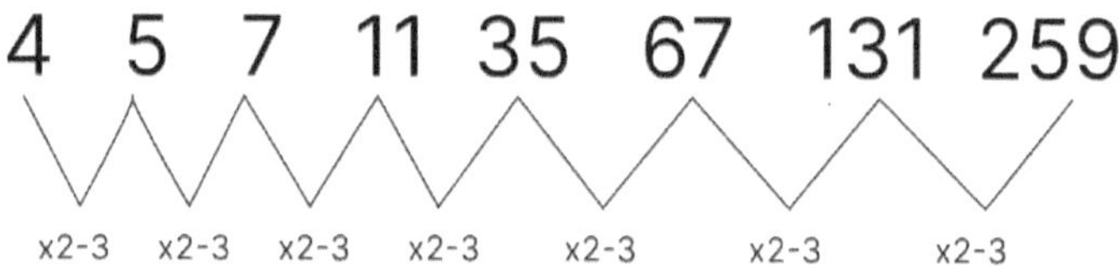

Write the missing term 67 in blank

27. ***Write in increasing order***

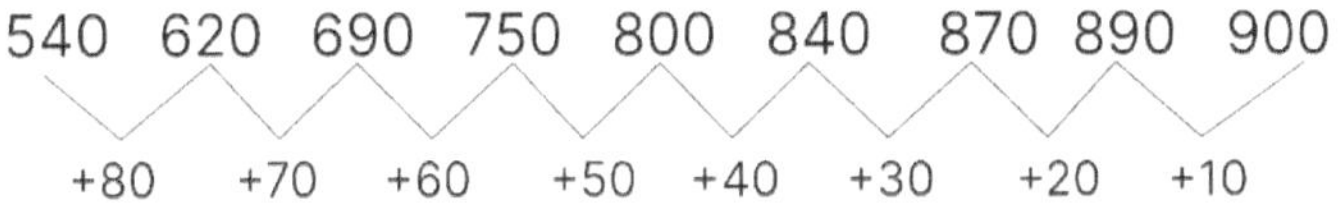

Write the missing term 840 in blank

28. ***Write in increasing order***

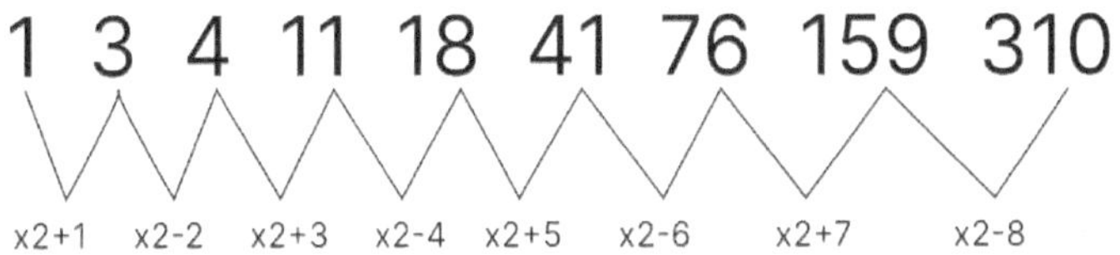

Write the missing term 76 in blank

29. ***Write in decreasing order***

Write the missing term 697 in blank

30. ***Write in increasing order***

2	3	10	15	26	35	50	63	83
1^2+1	2^2-1	3^2+1	4^2-1	5^2+1	6^2-1	7^2+1	8^2-1	9^2+1

Write the missing term 35 in blank

MATCHING SETS OF NUMBERS WITH ITS RULE

I.

1. 4 16 36 100 196

Rule (c) is followed In this manner

6 ---→ $6/3=2, 2^2=4$

12 ---→ $12/3=4, 4^2=16$

18 ---→ $18/3=6, 6^2=36$

30---→ $30/3= 10, 10^2=100$

42 ---→ $42/3=14, 14^2=196$

Sol: (c) →(1)

---

2. 33 138 315 885 1743

Rule (E) is followed in this manner

6 ---→ $6^2 - (6/2) =33$

12---→ $12^2 -(12/2) =138$

18---→ 18^2-**(18/2)**$=315$

30---→ $30^2-(30/2) =885$

42---→ $42^2-(42/2) =1743$

---

3. 8 11 14 20 26

Rule (A) is followed

6---→ (6/2) + 5 =8

12---→ (12/2) +5 =11

18---→ (18/2) + 5 =14

30---→ (30/2) + 5 = 20

42---→ (42/2) + 5 = 26

---

4. 32 142 322 898 1762

Rule (B) is followed

6 ---→ 6^2 – 2 =34

12---→ 12^2-2 =142

18---→ 18^2-2 = 322

30---→ 30^2- 2 = 898

42---→ 42^2 -2 =1762

---

5. 8 20 32 56 80

6 ---→ 2x6-4=8

12 ---→2x12 -4=20

18 ---→2x18- 4 =32

30 ---→ 2x 30-4 =56

42 ---→ 2x 42-4=80

Rule (D) is followed

II

1. 7, 21, 35, 49, 63

$2 \div 2 + 3 \times 2 = 7$

$6 \div 2 + 3 \times 6 = 21$

$10 \div 2 + 3 \times 10 = 35$

$14 \div 2 + 3 \times 14 = 49$

$18 \div 2 + 3 \times 18 = 63$

Sol.: (1) --> A

---

2. 1, 13, 25, 37, 49

$2 \times 3 - 5 = 1$

$6 \times 3 - 5 = 13$

$10 \times 3 - 5 = 25$

$14 \times 3 - 5 = 37$

$18 \times 3 - 5 = 49$

Sol.: (2) --> D

---

3. 1, 3, 5, 7, 9

$2 - 2 \div 2 = 1$

$6 - 6 \div 2 = 3$

$10 - 10 \div 2 = 5$

$14 - 14 \div 2 = 7$

$18 - 18 \div 2 = 9$

Sol.: (3) --> E

---

4. 5, 39, 105, 203, 333

$2^2 + 2 \div 2 = 5$

$6^2 + 6 \div 2 = 39$

$10^2 + 10 \div 2 = 105$

$14^2 + 14 \div 2 = 203$

$18^2 + 18 \div 2 = 333$

Sol.: (4) --> C

---

5. 3 5 7 9 11

$(2 + 4) \div 2 = 6 \div 2 = 3$

$(6 + 4) \div 2 = 10 \div 2 = 5$

$(10 + 4) \div 2 = 14 \div 2 = 7$

$(14 + 4) \div 2 = 18 \div 2 = 9$

$(18 + 4) \div 2 = 22 \div 2 = 11$

Ans (5) -> B

III

1. 0, 12, 32, 60, 96

$2^2 - 4 = 0$

$4^2 - 4 = 12$

$6^2 - 4 = 32$

$8^2 - 4 = 60$

$10^2 - 4 = 96$

Sol.: (1) --> E

---

2. 2, 12, 30, 56, 90

$2^2 - 2 = 2$

$4^2 - 4 = 12$

$6^2 - 6 = 30$

$8^2 - 8 = 56$

$10^2 - 10 = 90$

Sol.: (2) --> C

---

3. 5, 10, 15, 20, 25

$2 \times 5 \div 2 = 5$

$4 \times 5 \div 2 = 10$

$6 \times 5 \div 2 = 15$

$8 \times 5 \div 2 = 20$

$10 \times 5 \div 2 = 25$

Sol.: (3) --> B

---

4. 4, 32, 108, 256, 500

$2^3 \div 2 = 4$

$4^3 \div 2 = 32$

$6^3 \div 2 = 108$

$8^3 \div 2 = 256$

$10^3 \div 2 = 500$

Sol: (4) -> A

---

5. 5, 6, 7, 8, 9

$(2 + 8) \div 2 = 5$

$(4 + 8) \div 2 = 6$

$(6 + 8) \div 2 = 7$

$(8 + 8) \div 2 = 8$

$(10 + 8) \div 2 = 9$

Sol: (5) -> D

IV

1. 8, 34, 78, 140, 220

$3^2 - (3 \div 3) = 8$

$6^2 - (6 \div 3) = 34$

$9^2 - (9 \div 3) = 78$

$12^2 - (12 \div 3) = 140$

$15^2 - (15 \div 3) = 220$

Sol.: (1) --> C

---

2. 17, 206, 719, 1718, 3365

$3^3 - 10 = 17$

$6^3 - 10 = 206$

$9^3 - 10 = 719$

$12^3 - 10 = 1718$

$15^3 - 10 = 3365$

Sol.: (2) --> D

---

3. 7, 8, 9, 10, 11

$(3 \div 3) + 6 = 7$

$(6 \div 3) + 6 = 8$

$(9 \div 3) + 6 = 9$

$(12 \div 3) + 6 = 10$

$(15 \div 3) + 6 = 11$

Sol: (3) -> B

---

4. 14, 20, 26, 32,38

$(3 + 4) \times 2 = 14$

$(6 + 4) \times 2 = 20$

$(9 + 4) \times 2 = 26$

$(12 + 4) \times 2 = 32$

$(15 + 4) \times 2 = 38$

Sol: (4) -> E

---

5. 7,19,31,43,55

$(3 \times 4) - 5 = 7$

$(6 \times 4) - 5 = 19$

$(9 \times 4) - 5 = 31$

$(12 \times 4) - 5 = 43$

$(15 \times 4) - 5 = 55$

Sol: (5) -> A

V

1. 0, 8, 14, 48, 80

$2^2 - 2 \times 2 = 0$

$4^2 - 2 \times 4 = 8$

$6^2 - 2 \times 6 = 14$

$8^2 - 2 \times 8 = 48$

$10^2 - 2 \times 10 = 80$

Sol: (1) -> C

---

2. 0, 48, 192, 480, 960

$2^3 - 4 \times 2 = 0$

$4^3 - 4 \times 4 = 48$

$6^3 - 4 \times 6 = 192$

$8^3 - 4 \times 8 = 480$

$10^3 - 4 \times 10 = 960$

Sol.: (2) --> E

---

3. 5, 10, 15, 20, 25

$(2 \times 3) - (2 \div 2) = 5$

$(4 \times 3) - (4 \div 2) = 10$

$(6 \times 3) - (6 \div 2) = 15$

$(8 \times 3) - (8 \div 2) = 20$

$(10 \times 3) - (10 \div 2) = 25$

Sol.: (3) --> B

---

4. 1, 4, 9, 16, 25

$(2 \div 2)^2 = 1$

$(4 \div 2)^2 = 4$

$(6 \div 2)^2 = 9$

$(8 \div 2)^2 = 16$

$(10 \div 2)^2 = 25$

Sol.: (4) --> A

---

5. 7, 13, 19, 25, 31

$(2 \times 3) + 1 = 7$

$(4 \times 3) + 1 = 13$

$(6 \times 3) + 1 = 19$

$(8 \times 3) + 1 = 25$

$(10 \times 3) + 1 = 31$

Sol.: (5) --> D

VI

1. 7, 13, 19, 25, 31

$3 \times 2 + 1 = 7$

$6 \times 2 + 1 = 13$

$9 \times 2 + 1 = 19$

$12 \times 2 + 1 = 25$

$15 \times 2 + 1 = 31$

Sol.: (1) --> E

---

2. 1, 4, 9, 16, 25

$3^2 \div 9 = 1$

$6^2 \div 9 = 4$

$9^2 \div 9 = 9$

$12^2 \div 9 = 16$

$15^2 \div 9 = 25$

Sol.: (2) --> D

---

3. 4, 8, 12, 16, 20

$3 \times 4 \div 3 = 4$

$6 \times 4 \div 3 = 8$

$9 \times 4 \div 3 = 12$

$12 \times 4 \div 3 = 16$

$15 \times 4 \div 3 = 20$

Sol.: (3) --> C

---

4. 7, 14, 21, 28, 35

$3 \div 3 + 2 \times 3 = 7$

$6 \div 3 + 2 \times 6 = 14$

$9 \div 3 + 2 \times 9 = 21$

$12 \div 3 + 2 \times 12 = 28$

$15 \div 3 + 2 \times 15 = 35$

Sol.: (4) --> B

---

5. 12, 186, 684, 1668, 3300

$3^3 - 3 \times 5 = 12$

$6^3 - 6 \times 5 = 186$

$9^3 - 9 \times 5 = 684$

$12^3 - 12 \times 5 = 1668$

$15^3 - 15 \times 5 = 3300$

Sol.: (5) --> A

VII

1. 0, 18, 68, 150, 264

$(0 \div 2) + 0^2 = 0$

$(4 \div 2) + 4^2 = 18$

$(8 \div 2) + 8^2 = 68$

$(12 \div 2) + 12^2 = 150$

$(16 \div 2) + 16^2 = 264$

Sol.: (1) --> B

---

2. -9, 55, 503, 1719, 4087

$0^3 - 9 = -9$

$4^3 - 9 = 55$

$8^3 - 9 = 503$

$12^3 - 9 = 1719$

$16^3 - 9 = 4087$

Sol.: (2) --> E

---

3. 5, 7, 9, 11, 13

$(0 \div 2) + 5 = 5$

$(4 \div 2) + 5 = 7$

$(8 \div 2) + 5 = 9$

$(12 \div 2) + 5 = 11$

$(16 \div 2) + 5 = 13$

Sol.: (3) --> D

---

4. 4, 6, 8, 10, 12

$(0 + 8) \div 2 = 4$

$(4 + 8) \div 2 = 6$

$(8 + 8) \div 2 = 8$

$(12 + 8) \div 2 = 10$

$(16 + 8) \div 2 = 12$

Sol.: (4) --> A

---

5. 0, 4, 16, 36, 64

$0^2 \div 4 = 0$

$4^2 \div 4 = 4$

$8^2 \div 4 = 16$

$12^2 \div 4 = 36$

$16^2 \div 4 = 64$

Sol.: (5) --> C

VIII

1. 7, 21, 35, 49, 70

$(2 \div 2) \times 7 = 7$

$(6 \div 2) \times 7 = 21$

$(10 \div 2) \times 7 = 35$

$(14 \div 2) \times 7 = 49$

$(20 \div 2) \times 7 = 70$

Sol.: (1) --> C

---

2. 0, 16, 64, 144, 324

$(2 - 2)^2 = 0$

$(6 - 2)^2 = 16$

$(10 - 2)^2 = 64$

$(14 - 2)^2 = 144$

$(20 - 2)^2 = 324$

Sol.: (2) --> D

---

3. -2, 186, 950, 2674, 7900

$2^3 - 2 \times 5 = -2$

$6^3 - 6 \times 5 = 186$

$10^3 - 10 \times 5 = 950$

$14^3 - 14 \times 5 = 2674$

$20^3 - 20 \times 5 = 7900$

Sol.: (3) --> E

---

4. 2, 10, 26, 50, 101

$(2 \div 2)^2 + 1 = 2$

$(6 \div 2)^2 + 1 = 10$

$(10 \div 2)^2 + 1 = 26$

$(14 \div 2)^2 + 1 = 50$

$(20 \div 2)^2 + 1 = 101$

Sol.: (4) --> B

---

5. 6, 42, 110, 210, 420

$2^2 + 2 = 6$

$6^2 + 6 = 42$

$10^2 + 10 = 110$

$14^2 + 14 = 210$

$20^2 + 20 = 420$

Sol.: (5) --> A

COLOURING AND CUTTING OF CUBES

1.

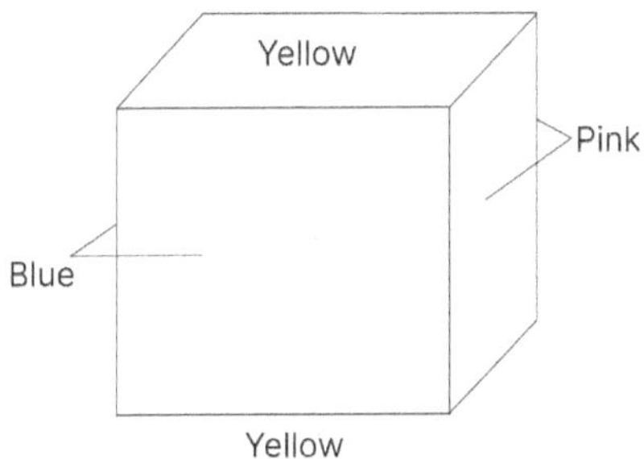

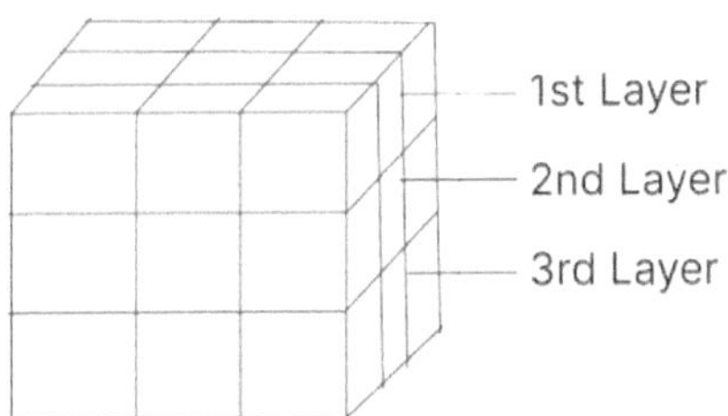

a. The whole of 2nd layer smaller cubes have none of their faces as yellow. So 9 smaller cubes of none yellow faces 3 (3).

b. (1) 15 of smaller cubes have at least one face as blue

c. (1) 12

d. (4) 6

e. (4) 18

2.

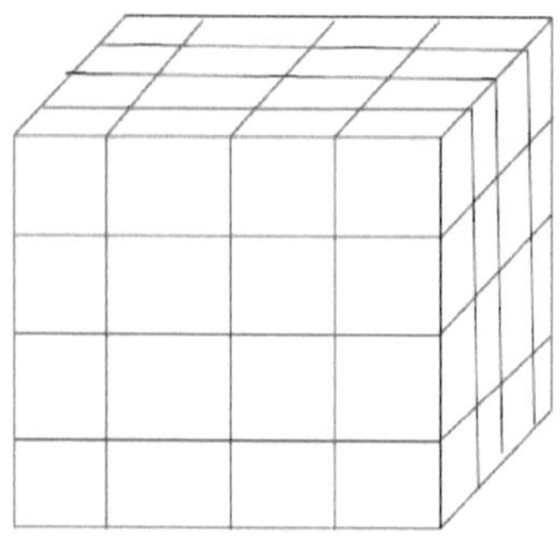

a. (2) 8

b. (1) 24

c. (3) 8

d. (2) 8

3.

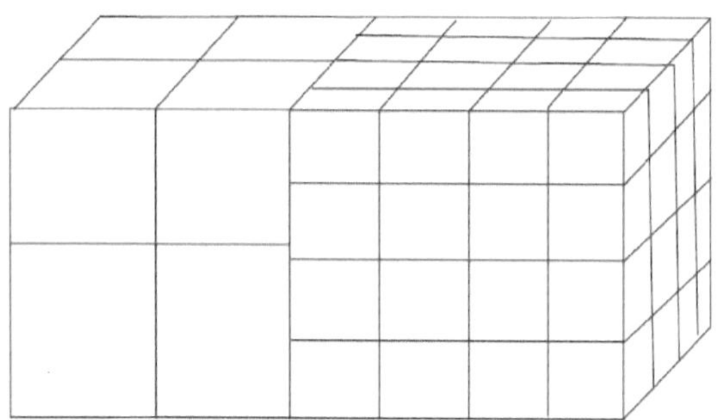

a. (2) 12

b. (4) 28

c. (4) 8

4.

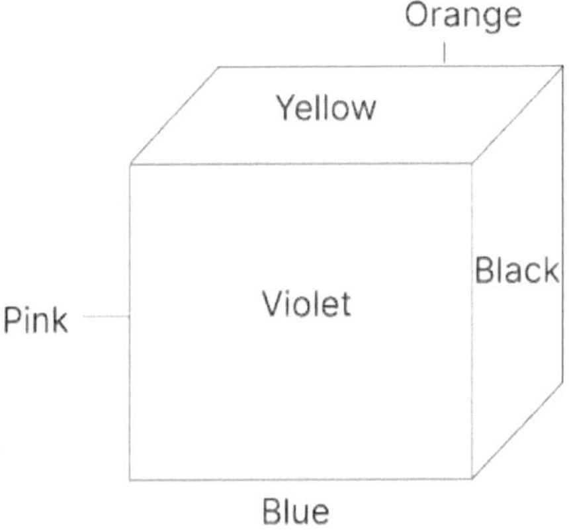

1. (d) Orange
2. (a) Pink
3. (b) Yellow
4. (c) Violet, Orange, Yellow, Blue

5.

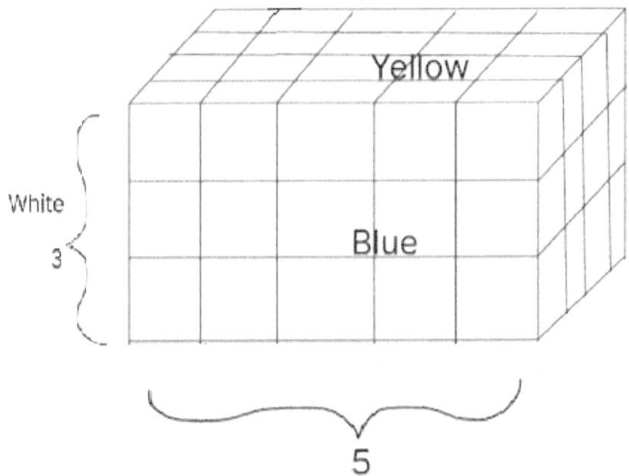

a. (3) 15

b. (2) 4

c. (4) 4

d. (3) 3

6.

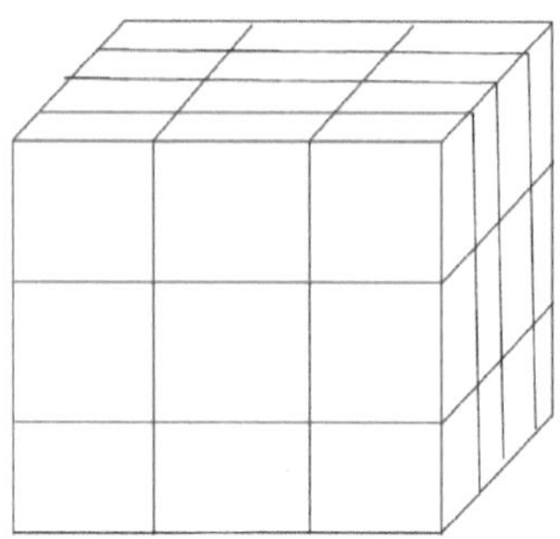

a. (1) 1

b. (4) 8

c. (3) 12

d. (4) 6

7.

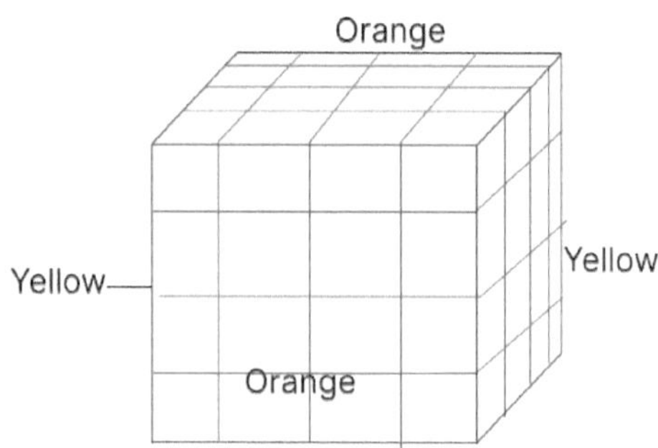

a. (3) 3

b. (1) 12

c. (3) 6

ANALYTICAL REASONING

I) The tabular column is as below

	PROFESSORS					SPORTS				
	Arch	Cont	Teach	Judge	Soft engg	Foot ball	Chess	Carom	Badmi nton	Swimm ing
P	X	✓	X	X	X	X	✓	X	X	X
Q	✓	X	X	X	X	✓	X	X	X	X
R	X	X	X	✓	X	X	X	✓	X	X
S	X	X	X	X	✓	X	X	X	✓	X
T	X	X	✓	X	X	X	X	X	X	✓

Answer seeing the tabular column

1. C) S
2. C) judge
3. A) Q
4. C) R
5. B) contractor

II)

	PROFESSOR					WIFE'S PROFESSION				
	Lecturer	Auditor	Dentist	Engg 1	Engg 2	Dentist	Teacher	Art	Dance	Sing
Rahul	x	✓	x	x	x	x	✓	x	x	x
Kumar	✓	x	x	x	x	x	x	x	✓	x
Satish	x	x	x	✓	x	x	x	x	x	✓
Anand	x	x	✓	x	x	✓	x	x	x	x
Sujay	x	x	x	x	✓	x	x	✓	x	x

Answer seeing tabular column

6. D) Anand
7. A) Rahul
8. D) Engineer
9. C) Kumar
10. B) Satish-singer

III)

	X	Y	Z	R	S	T	U
X							
Y				X			
Z						X	
R		X			X		
S				X			
T			X				
U							

Answer seeing tabular column

11. A)
12. B)
13. D)

IV)

	CAS						SINGLES					
	K	L	M	N	O	P	5	6	7	8	M	F
A									X	X		✓
B									X	X		✓
C			X	X	X						✓	
D			X	X	X						✓	
E			X	X	X						✓	
M	✓	✓				✓			✓	✓		
F			✓	✓	✓		✓	✓				

Answer seeing tabular column

14. DE and MN cannot happen at same time so (b) is not possible. Sol: b) DE,78,MN
15. D and MNO cannot be teams so © DA,7,MNO is not possible. Sol: c) DA,7,MNO
16. Sol: d) CDE,8,KL
17. Sol: a) AB,M,56
18. Sol: b) AB,NO,78

V) Let bangle 5 weigh =x

Bangle 4 weigh= x/2

Bangle3 weigh=(1/2)(x/2)=x/4

Bangle 2 weighs = (9/2)(x/4)=9x/8

Bangle 1 weighs= 2(9x/8)=9x/4

B5	B4	B3	B2	B1
X,	x/2,	x/4,	9x/8,	9x/4

Make everything have common denominator 8

8x/8, 4x/8, 2x/8, 9x/8, 18x/8

19. Descending order of weighs

18x/8,	9x/8,	8x/8	4x/8,	2x/8
B1,	B2,	B5,	B4	B3

Sol: (e) 1,2,5,4,3

20. B5 is lighter than B1 and B2

    Sol: (b) 1,2

21. B3 is least weighed

    Sol: (c) bangle 3

22. B1 is heaviest

    Sol: (a) bangle 1

23. Bangle 5 is heavier than B4 and B3

    Sol: (b) 4,3

CUBE FOLDING

1. 'a' and 'f' come at the end of ┐└. 'b' is alternate to square 'd'. 'c' is in square alternate to 'e'. So they form opposite.
Ans (c)

2. 1 & 3 are alternate blocks, 2 & 5 are alternate, so are 4 & 6 which are alternate blocks.
Ans (a)

3. △ & ⏢ are at the end of the ┐└ . O & ☐ are at the end of the └┐ .
☐ & ▱ are at the end of the ┐└ .
Ans (b)

4. N & R are at the end of the ┐└. M & P are alternate blocks. O & Q are alternate blocks.
Ans (d)

5. + & / are alternate blocks, * & % are alternate blocks, - & x are alternate blocks.
Ans (a)

6. ⬚ & ⬚ are at the end of the ┌┘. ⬚ & ⬚ are alternate blocks.
Ans (b)

7. S & U are alternate blocks. V & X are alternate blocks. T & W are at the end of the └┐ .
Ans (d)

8. 10 & 13 are at the end of the └┐ . 11 & 14 are at the end of the ┐└ .
12 & 15 are at the end of the └┐ .
Ans (d)

9. M & N are alternate blocks. I & K are alternate blocks. J & L are alternate blocks.
Ans (b)

10. ∩ & U are alternate blocks. • & < are alternate blocks. > & = are alternate blocks.
Ans (a)

11. P & R are alternate blocks. S & U are alternate blocks. Q & T are at the end of the ┐└ .
Ans (c)

DIRECTIONAL TESTS

1. Let 'S' be starting point and E be endpoint. The figure will be:

So, **ANS = 4 km**

2. Let 'S' be starting point and E be endpoint:

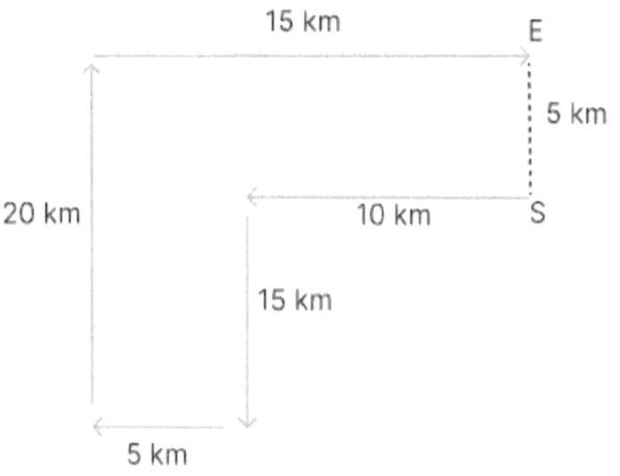

So, **ANS = 5 km**

3. Let's starting point and E be endpoint:

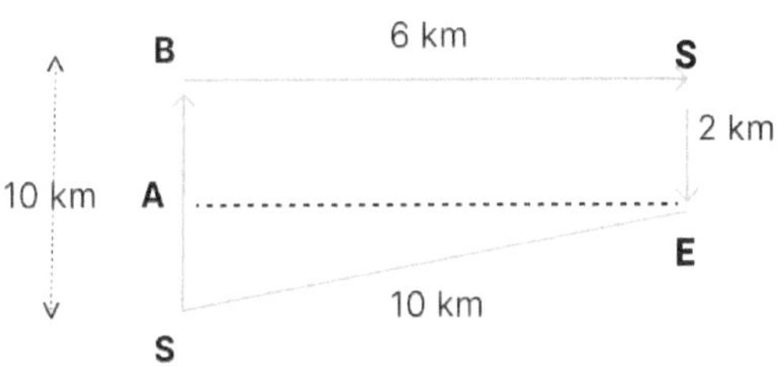

ANS-AE= 6km, BA= 2km

So, SA = 8 km by Pythagoras Theorem, SE = 10 km

4. Let S be starting point and E be endpoint:

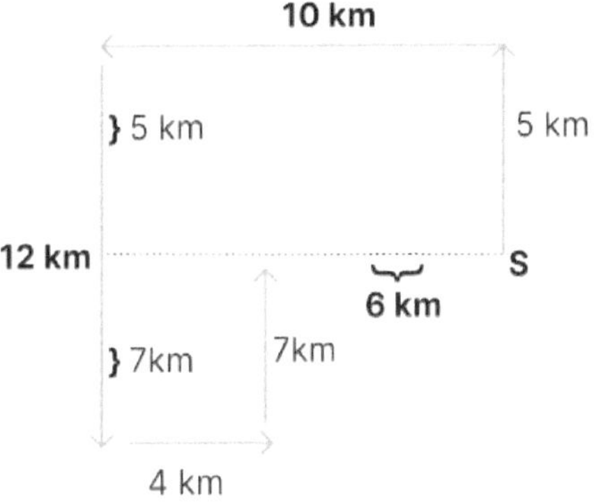

So, **ANS = 6 km**

5. The old position is:

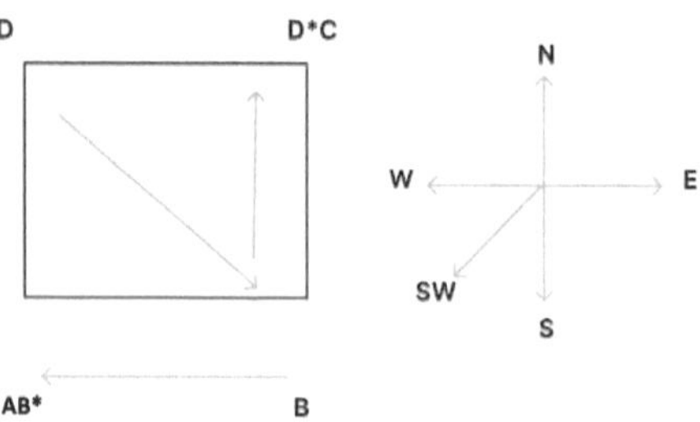

B* is the new position of B

So, B's new position is SW corner

ANS = C

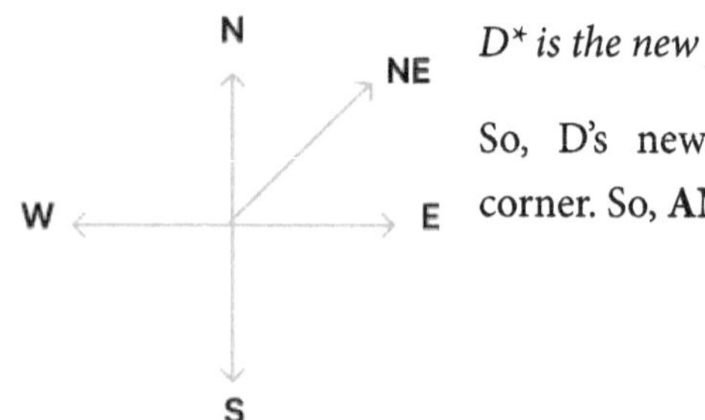

D is the new position of D*

So, D's new position is NE corner. So, **ANS = B**

6. Earlier positions

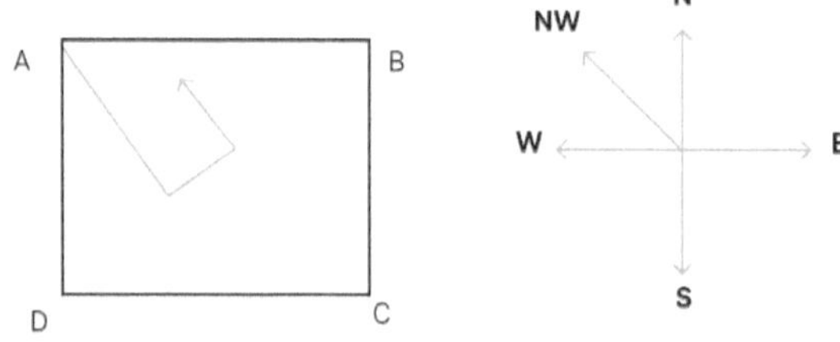

So, **Answer** = (b) NW

7. Old position is ABCD and the new one is repted by *:

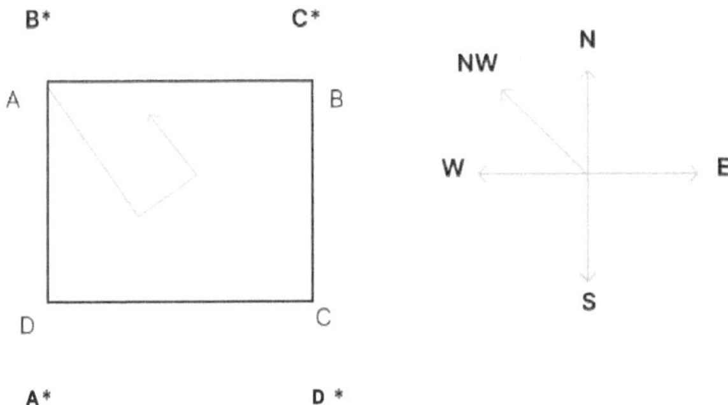

(1) ACBD is not a new arrangement

Answer: (c) ACBD

(2) B is newly located in NW corner

Answer: (b) NW corner

8. Starting point is S and endpoint is E

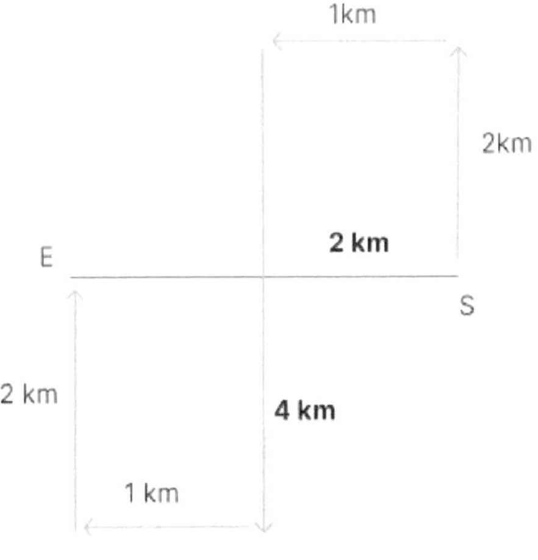

SE = 2km

Answer: (a) 2km

9. Option (b) is correct. **Answer = North**

10.

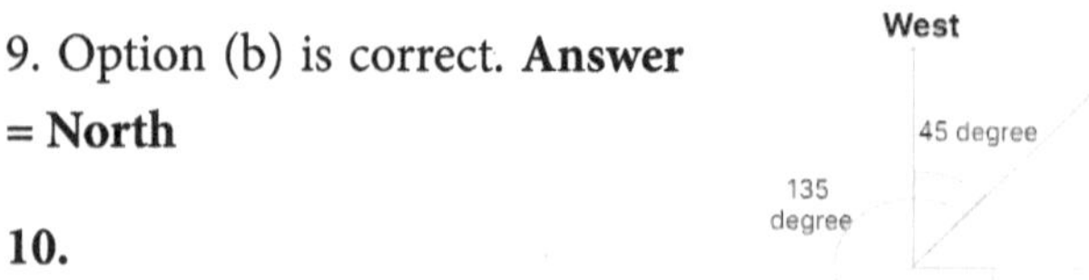

Answer = (c) North

11. A and B start at S.
Final position of A is E_A & B is E_B

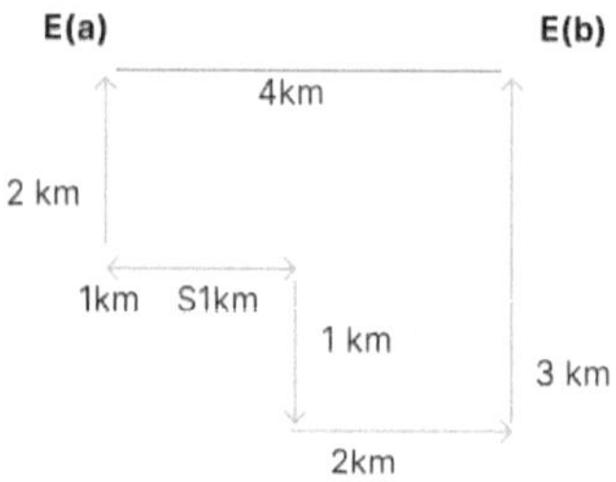

Final distance between A and B is 1+1+2=4km

Answer: (c) 4km

12. Let 2 cars start from A and B which are 120 km apart
E(A) is the endpoint of A, and E(B) is the endpoint of B

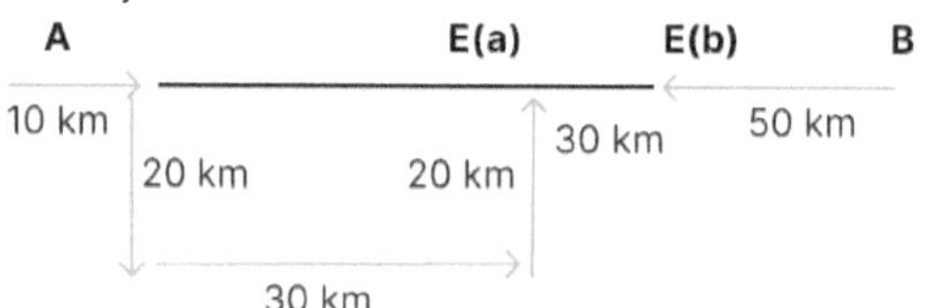

Answer: 30 km from E(a) to E(b)

13. At the beginning the woman was facing south

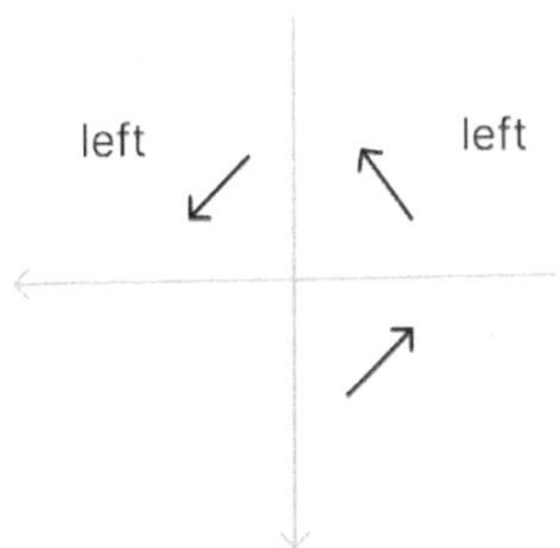

Answer: (a) South

14.

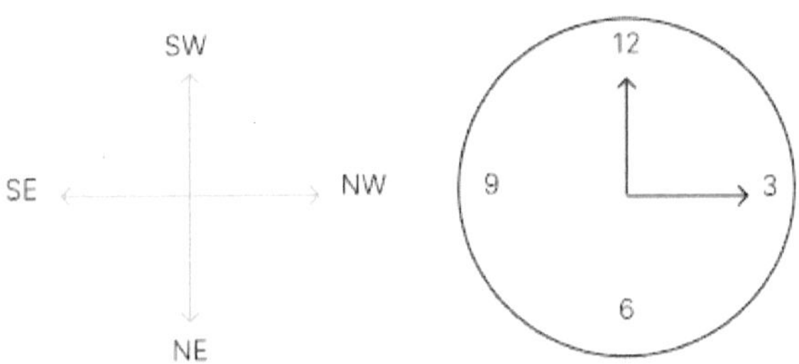

Answer: (b) NW

15. Earlier position are

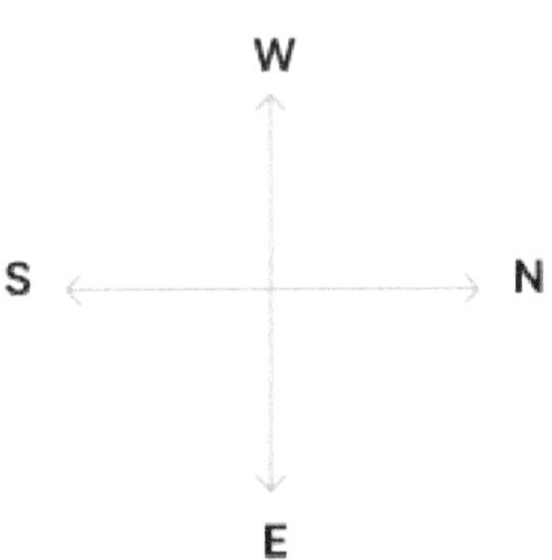

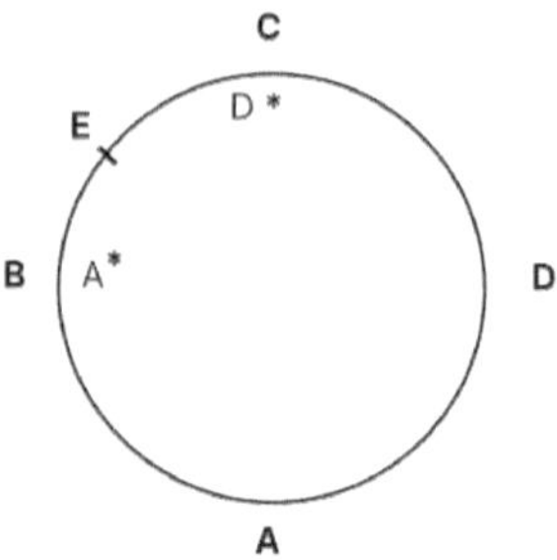

New position are given with *

Answer NW

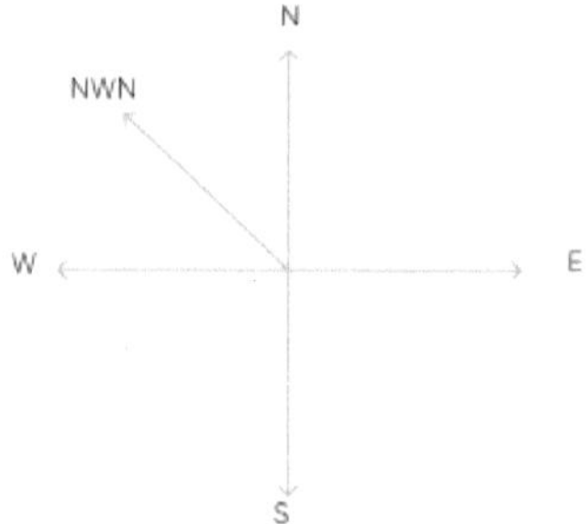

16. New position are given by:

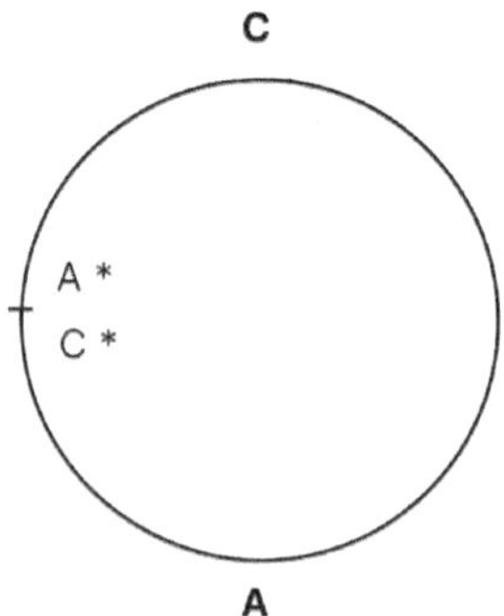

Answer: (B) 0 degree

17. New position are given by:

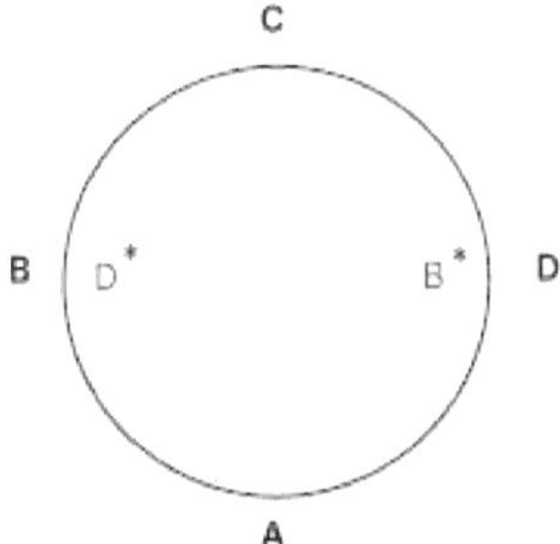

D is now in west direction

Answer: (d) west

18. New positions are given by:

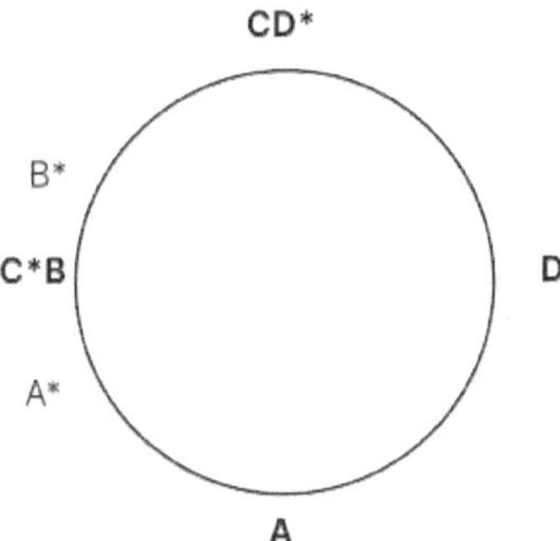

Clockwise new arrangement is ACBD

Answer: (a) ACBD

19. After drawing the landmarks with directions, we get:

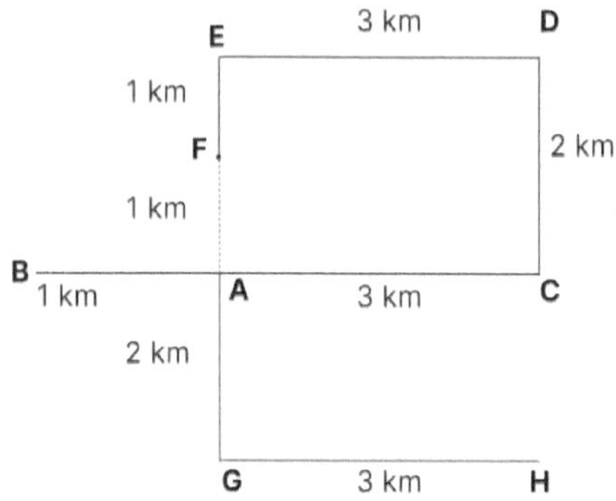

EFAG are in straight line

Answer: (d) EFAG

20. AG = 2 km, FA = 1km, so FG = AG + FA = 2 + 1 = 3km
So F is 3km north of G\

Answer: (a) 3KM north

CONSTRUCTION OF SQUARES AND TRIANGLES

When you put the 3 pieces together, it looks as below:

1.

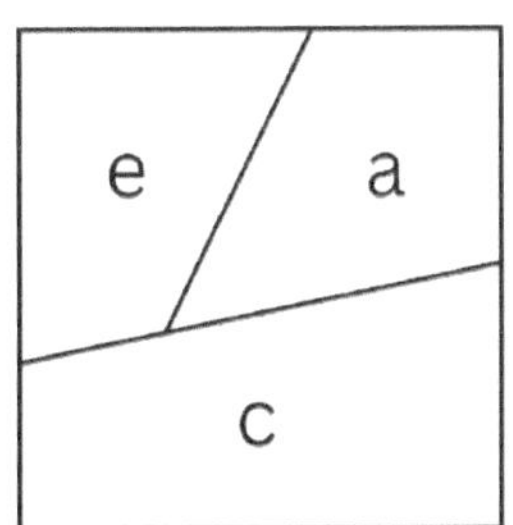

2.

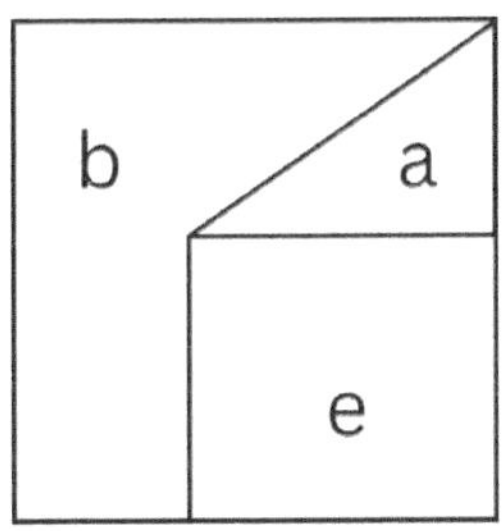

3.

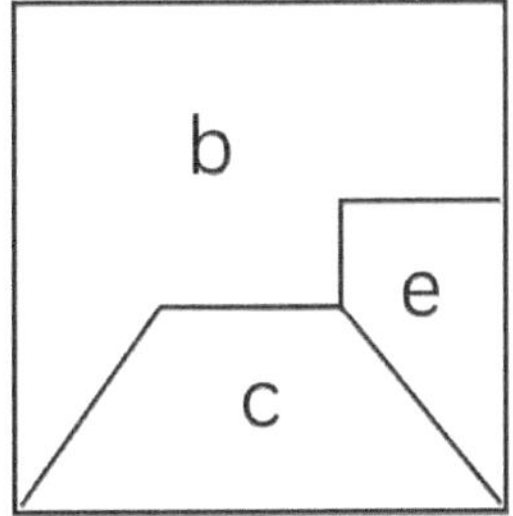

4.

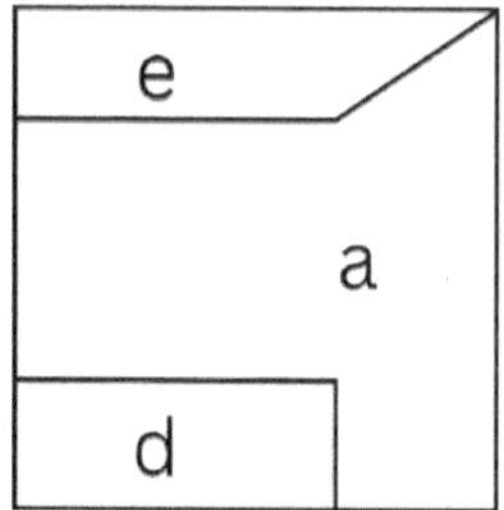

5.

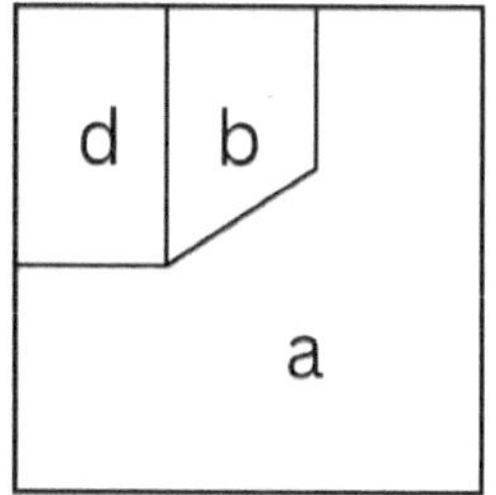

6.

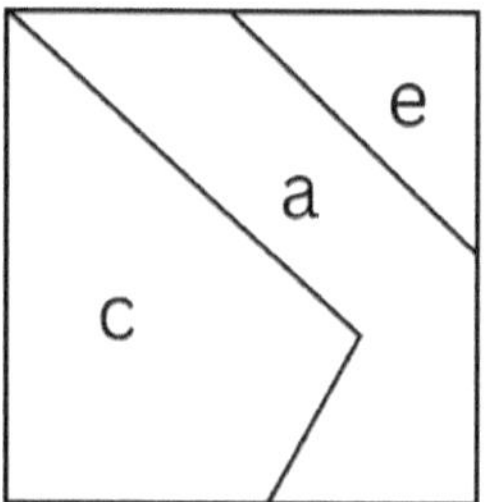

7.

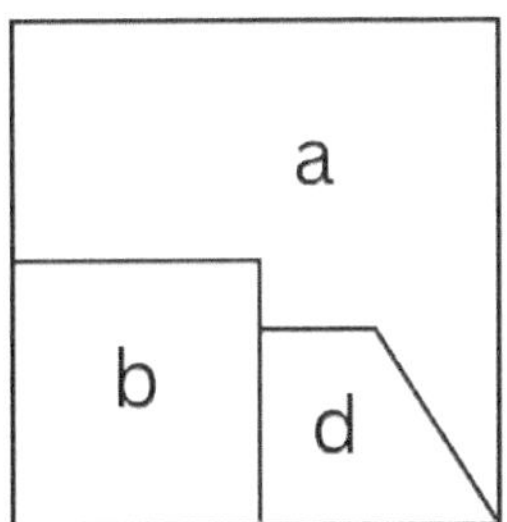

8.

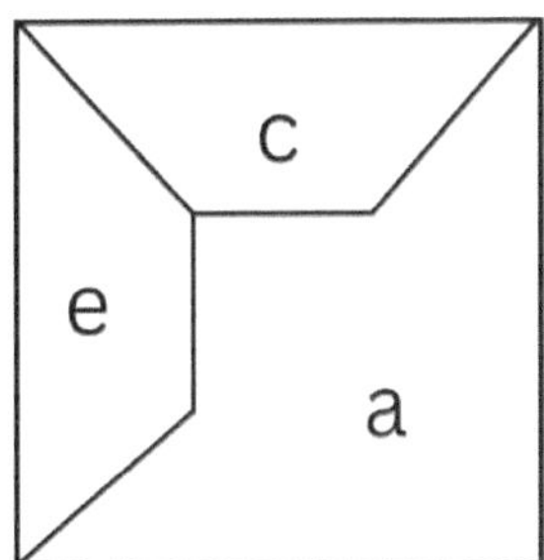

9.

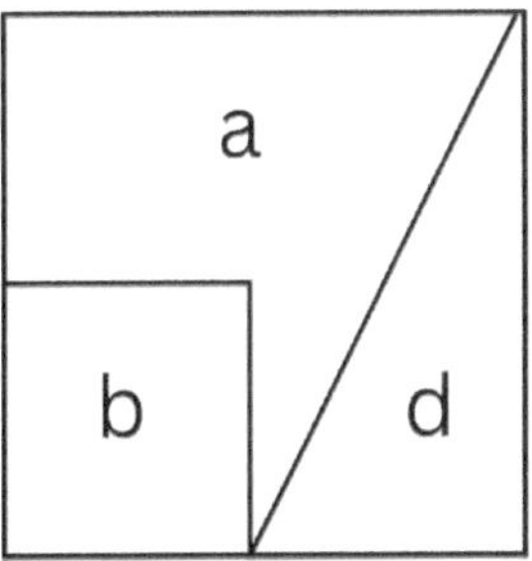

10.

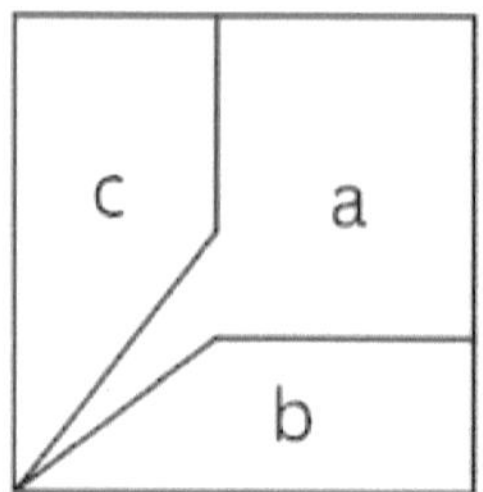

11.

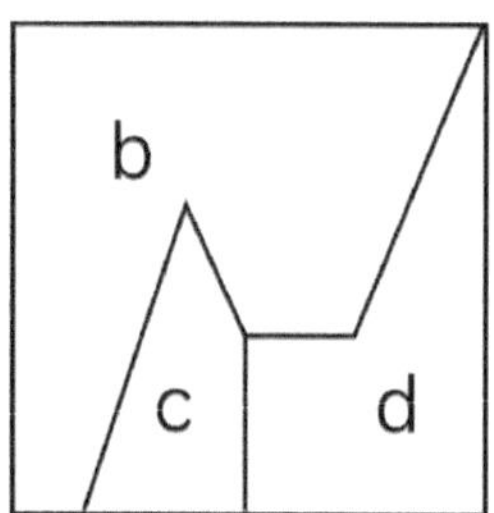

12.

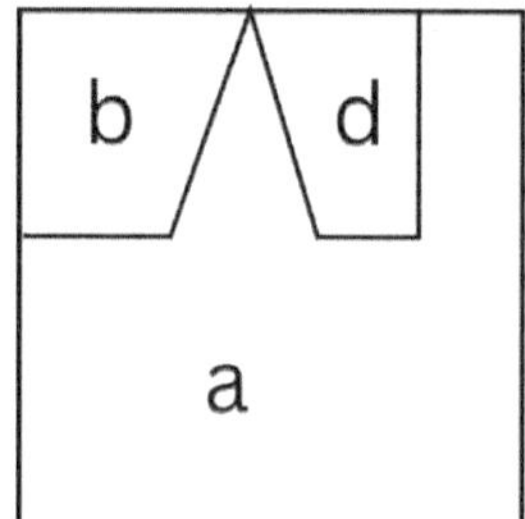

13.

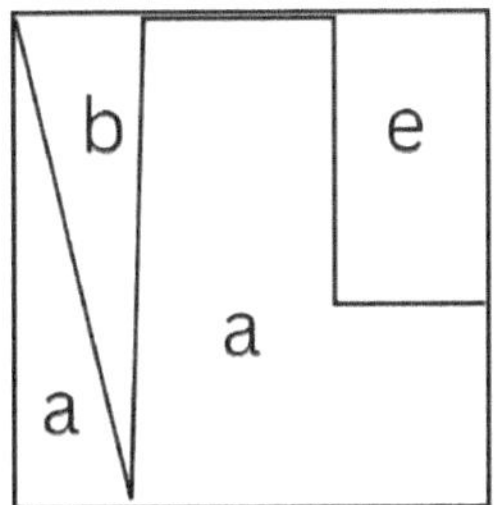

14.

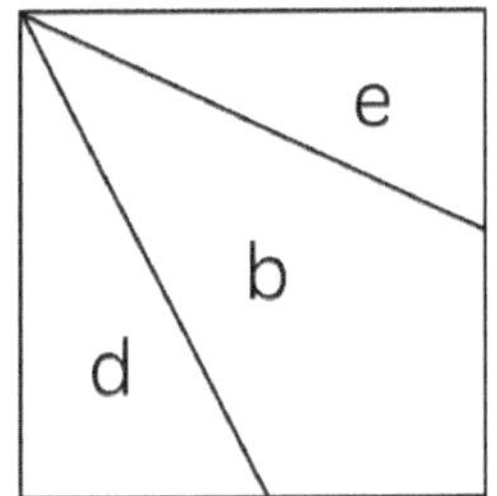

15.

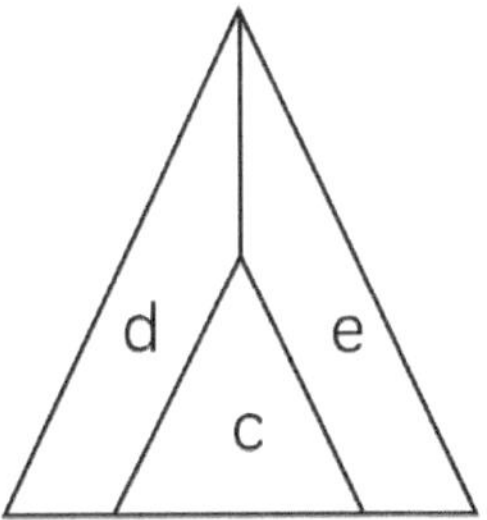

16.

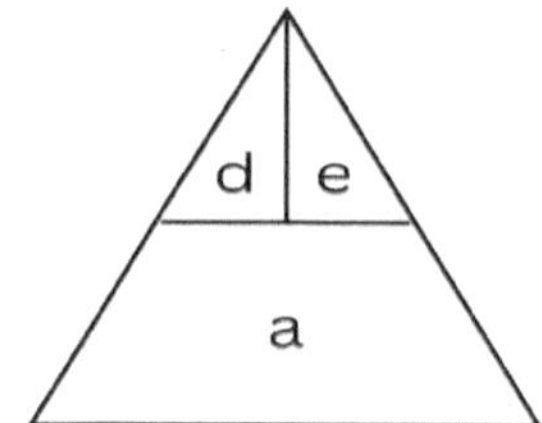

17.

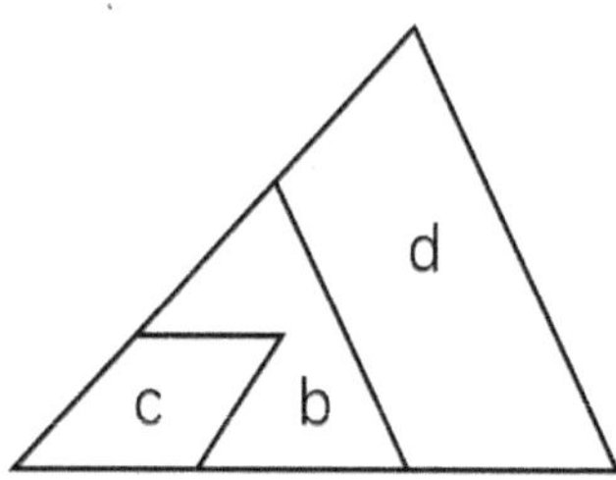

BRAIN TEASERS

1. Let the number of rabbits be x

Let the number of hens be y

$x + y = 79$

$\underline{4x + 2y = 266}$

$2x + 2y = 158$

$4x + 2y = 266$

Subtract

$-2x = -108$

$x = 54$

but $x + y = 79$

$54 + y = 79$

$Y = 25$

Therefore number of rabbits=54, number of hens=25

2. Let the 7 players be numbered 1,2,3,4,5,6,7

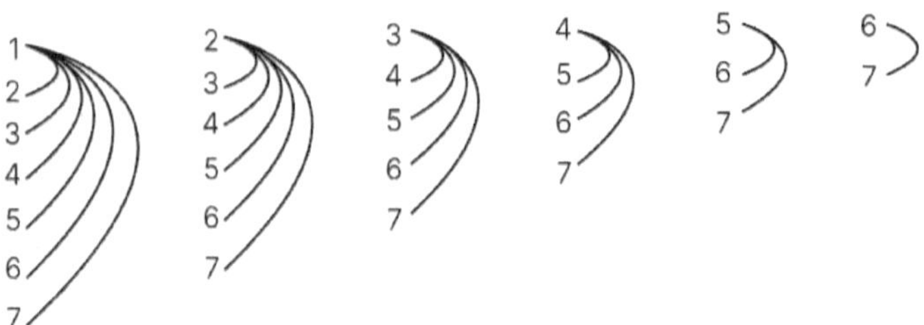

So total number of matches = 6+5+4+3+2+1= 21

3. Present ages

Let Raj's son's age = x

Therefore Raj 's age =7x

<u>After 10 years</u>

Raj's son's age = x +10

Raj's age=7x+10

According to problem

7x + 10 = 3 (x+10)

7x-3x=30-10

X=5

Raj's present age =7x5=35yrs

Raj's son's age=x=5yrs

4. Let the 2 digit number be= xy=10x+y

So reversed number will be= yx = 10y+x

X + y =13 ......(1)

Xy + 45 = yx

10x+y+45 =10y+x

X – y =-5 ......(2)

Solve for eq (1) and (2)

X + y =13

X – y =-5

2x = 8

X = 4

X + y = 13

4 + y = 13

Y = 9

So number is 49

5. On 1st day = 2 amoebas, 2^1=2

On 2nd day = 4 amoebas, 2^2=4

On 3rd day = 8 amoeba, 2^3=8

On x^{th} day= 256 amoebas, 2^x=256

X=8

So on 8th day, there are 256 amoebas

6. Let fraction be x/y

(x+1)/y=1 and x/(y+2)=1/2

X + 1 = y …….(1)

2x = y + 2 …….(2)

Put (1) in (2)

2x=x+1+2

X = 3

Y=x+1

Y=4

Fraction= ¾

7. Given number of buses = 1200

6xNumber of taxies = number of buses

Number of taxies=1200/6=200

5x number of autos= number of taxies

Number of autos= 200/5=40

4x number of cycles= number of autos

Number of cycles=40/4=10

8. Let the number of pens = x

Let the number of pencils = y

$5x + 3y = 41$

$8x + 1y = 58$

$5x + 3y = 41$

$24 + 3y = 174$

Subtract

$-19x=-133$

$X = 7$

$5x + 3y = 41$

$5(7) + 3y = 41$

$Y = 2$

9. If 2 tanjore painting costs =75600

1 tanjore painting will cost = 75600/2 = 37800

27x lippan paintings =6 tanjore paintings costs

1 lippan painting costs = (6x37800)/27=8400

9 mandala paintings = 21 lippan paintings

1 mandala will cost = 21x 8400/9=19600

3 water color paintings = 12 mandalas

1 water color paintings= 12x19600/3

1 water color painting = 78,400

10. Perimeter of triangle = 8x3 =24

Perimeter of square = 24 =4l

l = 24/4 = 6cm

Length of square = 6cm

11. Speed of train x = 400/5=80km/hr

Speed of train Y = 80+20 =100 km/hr

For train Y, speed = Distance/time

100=400/time

Time= 400/100 = 4 hrs

Time taken by train Y is 4 hrs

12. Let the weight of juice =x

The weight of bottle=170

(1x/3)+170=380

1x/3=380-170

1x/3=210

X = 630

Weight of juice = 630 gms

Weight of bottle filled with juice = 630+170=800gms

13. A monkey eats 1 banana 1st day, 3 bananas 2nd day, 5 bananas 3rd day…….so on

On 15th day, it would have eaten = 1 + 3 + 5 + 7……..=15^2=225

14.

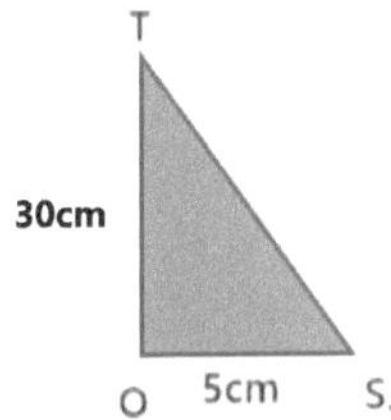

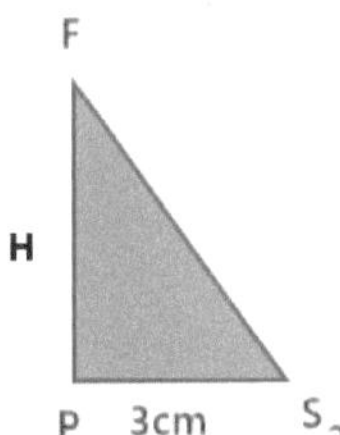

30/5 =h/3

h = 6x3

h=18m

15. Let length = l

Let breadth = b

(l + 2) (b – 2) = A -16

(l – 4) (b + 2) =A – 16

Lb - 2l + 2b – 4 = lb - 16

-l+b= -6 ………..(1)

Lb +2l -4b -8 = lb -16

L-2b=-4 ……….(2)

Consider eq(1) and (2)

$-l + b = -6$

$+l - 2b = -4$

$-1b = -10$

b=10

-l+10=-6

L = 16cm

16. Let number of apples = x

Therefore guavas = x – 6

Also oranges = x + 7

Total fruits are x + x – 6 + x + 7 =211

$3x + 1 = 211$

$X = 70$

Guavas = 70-6 =64

Oranges = 70+ 7 = 77

17. Let the total number of vegetables be x

10% are rotten and throw away = x/10

Remaining is = x – (x/10)= 9x/10

40% of remaining are rotten and throw =(9x/10)x(40/100)

=9x/25

Rotten and thrown away vegetables are = (x/10) +(9x/25)

=23x/50

=46%

Sol: 46%

18. LCM of 5,6,7 = 210

Pack had 210+2=212 chocolates

19. There are

2 black kings in a pack of cards

Total number of cards = 52

Proability that a person picks a black king = (2/52)=1/26

20. Let the number of times he hits the mark = x

So the number of times he misses the mark = 60 – x

0.50x -0.20 (60-x) =1.30

0.70x = 13.30

X = 19

He hit 19 times

21. Let the 2 digit number be = xy = 10x +y

Reverse of the number is = yx = 10y + x

According to problem,

X = 2y + 2 ....(1)

And 10y + x = 5 +3x +3y

7y = 5 +2x ....(2)

Substitute (1) in (2)

7y =5 + 2 (2y+2)

Y = 3

X = 2y + 2

X = 8

Sol: 83

22. Let Ajit have = Rs x

Let Ram have = Rs y

X + 100 = 2(y -100)

X = 2y – 300 ....(1)

Also,

6(x – 10) = y +10

6x - y = 70 ....(2)

Put eq (1) in (2)

6 (2y -300) – y =70

Y = 170

X = 2y – 300

X = 40

23. Let the age of B = x

Therefore the age of A = x +2

Also age of D, A's father = 2(x+2)

B's sister, C' s age = x/2

According to problem,

2(x +2) – x/2 = 40

X = 24

B's age = 24

A's age = 26

www.ingramcontent.com/pod-product-compliance
Lightning Source LLC
LaVergne TN
LVHW090121160826
845673LV00015B/373